101 Comedy Games
for Children and Grown-Ups

SmartFun Activity Books from Hunter House

Ordering

Trade bookstores in the U.S. and Canada please contact

Publishers Group West

1700 Fourth Street, Berkeley CA 94710

Phone: (800) 788-3123   Fax: (800) 351-5073

For bulk orders please contact

Special Sales

Hunter House Inc., PO Box 2914, Alameda CA 94501-0914

Phone: (510) 899-5041   Fax: (510) 865-4295

E-mail: sales@hunterhouse.com

Individuals can order our books by calling **(800) 266-5592**

or from our website at **www.hunterhouse.com**

101
Comedy Games
for Children
and Grown-Ups

Leigh Anne Jasheway

A Hunter House SmartFun Book

*Thanks to all the kids, both young and old, who have reminded me
every day about how important laughter and play are
in living a healthy and happy life.*

Hunter House Inc., Publishers
PO Box 2914
Alameda CA 94501-0914

Library of Congress Cataloging-in-Publication Data
Jasheway-Bryant, Leigh Anne.
101 comedy games for children and grown-ups / Leigh Anne Jasheway.
pages cm. — (SmartFun activity books)
ISBN 978-0-89793-700-9 (pbk.) —ISBN 978-0-89793-701-6 (spiral)
ISBN 978-0-89793-703-0 (ebk.)
1. Games—Juvenile literature.   2. Comedy—Juvenile literature.   3. Comedy sketches—
Juvenile literature.   4. Creative activities and seat work—Juvenile literature.   I. Title.   II. Title:
One hundred one comedy games for children and grown-ups.   III. Title: One hundred and one
comedy games for children and grown-ups.
GV1203.J35 2014
790.1′922—dc23   2013034080

Project Credits

Cover Design: Jinni Fontana Rights Coordinator: Candace Groskreutz
Book Production: John McKercher Customer Service Manager:
Developmental and Copy Editor: Amy Bauman   Christina Sverdrup
Managing Editor: Alexandra Mummery Order Fulfillment: Washul Lakdhon
Publicity Coordinator: Martha Scarpati Administrator: Theresa Nelson
Special Sales Manager: Judy Hardin IT Support: Peter Eichelberger
Publisher: Kiran S. Rana

Printed and bound by Bang Printing, Brainerd, Minnesota
Manufactured in the United States of America

9 8 7 6 5 4 3 2 1   First Edition   14 15 16 17 18

Contents

Introduction
Laughing Out Loud:
Why a Chuckle and a Snort Are So Much Fun

The Games
Finding Your Inner Funny

A list of the games, divided by age groups, begins on the next page.
Please note that, while the photographs in this book show limited diversity,
this book is for people of all races and ethnic identities.

List of Games

(Including Some Bonus High-Tech Games)

Preface

Although my inner child insists it can't be true, I've been teaching all kinds of comedy games for almost twenty years. Whether writing comedy or doing stand-up, sketch comedy, or improv, I've never had more fun than when playing with groups of kids and grown-ups who let their inner children out to have fun. I've taught comedy to middle schoolers in a school gym, to corporate business-types in ties and pantyhose (not on the same individuals, although that would be fun), to whoever shows up at my evening community college comedy classes, to retirees in nursing homes.... I once taught comedy at a Mennonite home with a helper monkey as an assistant. Nothing encourages people to have fun like a monkey in the room!

Here's the thing: I wasn't voted class clown in high school. Had there been such a choice, I'd probably have been voted Most Likely to Depress People. My role models were Sylvia Plath and Edgar Alan Poe. To say I was a serious child is to say a hurricane is breezy. But in my early thirties, I accidentally signed up for a comedy class, and it changed everything about my life—I became a happier, healthier, saner, and more fun person to be around. This is why I've spent so much time trying to help others make this discovery for themselves. Not only is laughter and play fun, it's vital to our survival. Nothing works better at releasing stress and fear than a good belly laugh. And if you can create that for yourself, whether you're five or eighty-five, you're going to be a lot more resilient.

Back when I was twelve—or even twenty-two—I would have agreed with the statement, "Some people are just born without a sense of humor" because I seemed to be one of them. But now I know better—not only from personal experience but also from research into the development of sense of humor in babies and children. Did you know the following?

- Babies' first non-gas-related laugh happens when they're approximately three months old.

- The reason toddlers laugh at peek-a-boo is because when Mom or Dad temporarily disappears, it scares them, and when he or she reappears, they're so relieved that the laughter naturally erupts.

- Knock-knock jokes and riddles are a good way to track a child's development of language skills.

- The types of things that make us laugh as adults—wordplay, scatological humor, physical comedy, prop comedy, music, etc.—start tickling our funny bones before we reach high school.

Even people who haven't laughed in so long that there's dinosaur dust on their funny bones can learn to be funny. After all, I was thirty-two the first time I took to a stand-up comedy stage. And I've had students aged seven to eighty-three perform comedy after taking one of my classes. There was eleven-year-old Matt, who, after just moving in with his seventh foster family, wrote this joke: "I love my new dad. He's bald, so when we go to the movies, he sits in front of us, and we watch the movie off the top of his head." And sixty-seven-year-old John who did this joke as part of a stand-up show he performed in not long after having a stroke, "After my stroke, they took away my driver's license, but they forgot to take away my forklift license. If anyone needs anything moved, that's my forklift in the handicapped zone outside."

Anyone can do comedy because we all have funny inside us. All it takes is a willingness to allow our playful spirit to be in charge once in a while. The games in this book cover the comedy gamut—from writing jokes and scenes to creating funny facial expressions and body movements to improv to stand-up. You will even find some high-tech comedy games. All of these games can be used for groups of kids (I recommend kids age 7 and up) or groups of big kids (age 17 and up). Although you may use them for kids and big kids together, because so much of comedy depends on our point of view and references, it's usually easier to work with kid groups and big-kid groups separately.

I love teaching comedy, and I'm sure you will, too. It combines bringing joy and laughter to others with teaching life skills that may have a permanent positive effect on the lives of others. Really, what's not to love? But, you may be asking, what if I don't trust my own comedy skills? Not to worry; most of the games in this book have prompts or lists so you don't have to come up with comedy suggestions all by yourself. And once you feel that you've developed your funny legs, you can add your own ideas to the list.

This book is divided into chapters by types of comedy: The content includes sections on breaking the ice, physical comedy, comedy writing, stand-up comedy, sketch comedy, improv, musical comedy, prop comedy, and high-tech comedy. You can focus on a different element of comedy every time your group meets or mix and match to explore a little bit of everything. As long as everyone keeps laughing, there is no *wrong* way to use this book…except, of course, to use it to level out the legs of your desk!

Introduction

Laughing Out Loud:
Why a Chuckle and a Snort
Are So Much Fun

Girls (and Boys
and Women and Men)
Just Wanna Have Fun

The one thing almost everyone has in common, no matter how young or old we are, is the desire to have fun and laugh. When we are very young (about five years old), we are experts in fun and know exactly what is required to have a day chock-full of it: make lots of friends and play often with them; forget about what other people (especially grown-ups) think; make up new games and new rules all of the time; concentrate on having fun now, not on whether it will have some "productive" use later; and when Mom says it's time to come inside, yell back, "But I'm not done having fun yet!"

Young American children laugh maybe a hundred times a day. I know this because I once got permission to follow a group of Head Start preschoolers around for an entire day and tracked how often they giggled. For the average American adult, laughter erupts only about fifteen times a day. (We may be texting "LOL" at the end of every text or tweet, but we're not really doing it.) The vast majority of things that cause children to laugh out loud aren't jokes or comedy routines. They do most of their laughing while playing—climbing trees, riding bikes, building sandcastles, playing tag, etc.—an activity older kids and adults forget how to do.

We can all learn a lot from our younger selves about becoming funnier and using our comedy skills to live a life filled with more fun and joy. The primary principles are these:

- Have a childlike playfulness and sense of wonder.
- Forget about what anyone else (including the voices in your head) may think.
- Use your brain, your heart, and your entire body to create laughter.
- Stop focusing on trying to be perfect and instead focus on trying to create fun for yourself and others.

It's important to keep in mind that whether it seems like it or not, everyone has a sense of humor. In fact, scientists now say that it's not just humans who have it; most mammals have a sense of humor and playfulness. Of course, we don't all laugh in the same way. (Just try getting a cat to chuckle, and you'll see what I mean.) But across the species, a sense of humor serves two important functions in life: It helps us release tension and fear, and it helps us bond with others.

Think about why television programming includes so many late night comedy shows. Why do so many people want to tune in to something that will make them laugh at the end of the day (and most likely after having just watched the news or a gory drama show)? It's the need to reduce the tension and fear of the day and to feel relaxed before going to bed. And the reason we love going out with our good friends—the ones who can make us laugh just by walking in a room—or going to comedy movies or stand-up shows with others is that we feel closer to people when we laugh with them. Consider this old saying: "Laughter is the shortest distance between people." Studies have found that we laugh a lot more when we're with people than when we're by ourselves; we want to share our laughter.

A Banana Peel, a Silly Word, and Two Marshmallows up the Nose: The Basic Ingredients for Funny

We know, of course, that different people laugh at different things, but guidelines definitely exist to help people who are trying to be funny do so. These "rules of comedy" have evolved from evaluating the types of topics or scenes that have made people laugh for hundreds (if not thousands) of years and trying to create formulas that mimic what naturally tickles our funny bone. We know, for example, that if we say, "My cat is sick," whomever we're talking with will express sympathy. We also know that if we say, "My cat scored higher than I did on last week's math test," we'll probably be rewarded with a giggle or a guffaw.

Three specific elements are almost always required to make strangers laugh. (Remember, we can usually make our friends laugh without having to work at it too hard. We have chemistry and history with our friends; strangers are another story altogether.) These required elements are:

- exaggeration
- misdirection
- incongruity

Exaggeration lets someone know that what you're saying or doing probably didn't happen in real life. Because of this, it helps provide distance from reality, which helps makes things funny. If a comedian decides to joke about a chronic disease he or she has, lots of exaggeration will be required to give the audience "permission to laugh." Without exaggeration, the jokes may come across as too painful or sad.

Exaggeration doesn't only apply to what we say when we're trying to be funny, but how we say it. In drama, actors are cautioned not to overplay their roles, to use subtlety and nuance instead. While these skills may also work for comedians, comedy also gives us permission to ham it up, to overact, and mug for the audience. Think about Robin Williams, Jim Carrey, Lily Tomlin, the Monty Python players, and everyone who has ever starred on *Saturday*

Night Live. Not only are the comedian's words exaggerated, but their physical motions, facial expressions, and vocal performances are exaggerated as well. Often even their costumes are exaggerated.

Misdirection, on the other hand, means that we don't see the funny part coming. With mystery writing, if you can guess who did it, there is no mystery; similarly, with comedy, if you can see the funny part coming, you're not going to laugh as much when it arrives.

A joke has two parts: the setup and the punch line. Another way to look at these components is as *pattern* and *misdirection*. And if you think about it, isn't life about thinking you're going in one direction and then winding up somewhere else? That's why so much of comedy is about real life annoyances and tragedies—breaking up with a girlfriend or boyfriend, not getting the job, failing a test, or accidentally walking into a sliding glass door, for example. Instead of whining or getting frustrated with the change in direction life takes, comedy teaches us to look for the funny in the misdirections in our lives.

The most important guidelines for using misdirection as a comedy tool is that the punch line always has to go at the end. The reason explaining a joke doesn't work is that the cat is already out of the bag—we've seen the misdirection, so there isn't any surprise left.

The third element is incongruity. Even toddlers understand this concept—call the cat "doggy" or the dog "daddy," and they will giggle. Incongruity creates laughter because our brains recognize that things don't belong together. But because they are together, they're funny. If you run into the Pope on a Segway in the grocery story buying star fruit, that's incongruous, and chances are, you'll crack up.

Although exaggeration and misdirection, and sometimes incongruity, can be interpreted as "lying," it's important to note that the more comedy starts from a place of honesty and personal truth, the stronger a connection the comedian makes with the audience. These tools of comedy help take the truth and make it funny enough that we release our stress, bond with each other, and laugh so hard that tears run down our legs.

Why Everyone
Should Be the Class Clown

We've already learned that natural and spontaneous laughter can help people reduce stress and feel a stronger connection with those around them. But what about those who write and perform comedy? What benefits do they get?

Performing comedy helps us:

1. Move past our fears. Once you've gotten up in front of a group of people and tried to make them laugh, you learn that taking risks can be fun—even if you do forget a joke, fall down, or trip over your own feet along the way. In fact, failing is a lot more fun in comedy because it can easily become part of the act.

2. Learn not to take everything in life so seriously. Playing comedy games is a good reminder that most of us, even children, turn everything into a bigger drama than it has to be. There's a reason that there's no such thing as stand-up tragedy; it's too much like what we do in our real lives.

3. Find the funny in life's misdirections instead of complaining, sitting in time out, throwing a temper tantrum, whining, feeling impatient or frustrated, kvetching, getting angry, holding a grudge, or punching a hole in the wall. While negative reactions to life's annoyances are natural and serve a function, holding onto anger can make us sick and tired.

4. Become better writers. With the exception of improv comedy, almost all types of comedy require you to write funny before you perform. For grown-ups, comedy writing is useful in everything from advertising to blogging to marketing that next big community fundraiser you're in charge of. For kids, the ability to write jokes and funny stuff can boost their popularity among their peers.

5. Play well with others. Improv and sketch comedy require that you focus on listening to others, becoming more flexible, and understanding that teams who laugh together tend to like working (or playing) together more than those who spend their time thinking of ways to make each others' lives miserable. This lesson pays off in almost any activity in life that you don't do alone.

6. Become more creative. You can't write a punch line or improvise something unexpected if your thinking is stuck in a rut. Using misdirection requires that you start thinking not only outside the box but also outside your own brain. Talk about a great way to shake the cobwebs off your cerebellum! Whether you're seven or seventy, boosting creativity is a great way to enjoy life a lot more.

7. Tap into our inner five-year-olds. Look at a five-year-old. Look at yourself. Now look back at the five-year-old. Who do you think enjoys life more?

Chief Court Jester
Job Description

If you're in charge of facilitating the funny games in this book, you can consider yourself the chief court jester (CCJ). The great thing about your job is that you get to have fun, too. If you don't model funny behavior, your players will be more serious than burned toast, so make sure you enter into your role with a strong sense of playfulness and a willingness to throw yourself into any activity to demonstrate and/or make a fool out of yourself before you ask anyone else to do the same.

In addition to clowning around, you should follow the basic guidelines below to make sure that each game works as effectively as it can.

Encourage participation. The players may originally have some hesitation about doing things that are silly and out of character. This is especially true for anyone between the ages of about fourteen and thirty-five, the ages during which we care most about what other people think about us, and for people who work together and are afraid that appearing foolish will somehow diminish their being taken seriously later. Let the performers know that getting past our fear of appearing foolish is part of having fun. Suggest that the more foolish they are when performing these games, the better job they are doing. Remind them that no one really succeeds without taking risks.

Ensure that everyone gets a turn. Often you will have a few players who want to jump into every game and monopolize the time and attention. It's up to you to make sure that everyone who wants to play gets a chance. Encourage those who are reluctant by making suggestions in the beginning for what they might add to a scene or exercise.

Make sure play moves forward. Once an exchange is no longer fun or funny for the players, the game is either over or needs a change in direction. Because the primary function of comedy games is to evoke laughter, the absence of snickers (no, not the candy bar) is a clear sign that the game isn't working or is finished. As CCJ, it is your job to pay attention to the laughter and be ready to step in to change things up or move on to a new game.

Be a laugh leader. Many players may be rusty when it comes to laughing out loud in a room full of strangers. It is part of your role to be an easy laugher so that you encourage others to join in. In comedy games, the gift of laughter is huge. You may want to practice beforehand if it's been awhile since you've heard the sound of your own laughter. Also, be the first to applaud for each individual or group following the end of a game.

Give players a license to "go there" but be prepared to put on the brakes. Comedy tends to get dirty, no matter what age group you're dealing with. The earliest emergence of potty humor starts for most children right around elementary school (which is also when basic wordplay, exaggeration, and slapstick become popular). In middle school, sexual humor becomes very popular. For many adults—males more than females—these types of humor continue to be front and center of what is funny to them. Being too restrictive can hamper the flow of ideas, but you can feel your group out in the beginning to see where they stand on these issues and stick to a general set of guidelines about scatological and sexual humor. (Also, see rules below for responding to individual players who have a problem with specific topics.)

Use basic rules to make sure that feelings are not hurt or toes stepped on (unless stepping on toes is done comedically). No one likes a bunch of rules, but to get everything started off on the right (or left) foot, it helps to review a few policies with the children or adult children you'll be working with.

Here's a script you might want to adapt for your class:

Everyone, before we get started, I want to give you some guidelines for making today's activities fun and funny for everyone:

1. **Have fun!** This is your chance to let loose and see how wild and wacky you can be. If you've ever wanted to try something out but thought it was too silly, here's your chance. When you hear those inner voices telling you that you'll look stupid or people will laugh at you, that's when you know you're on the right track!

2. **Be supportive of each other.** Humor can be fun for everyone as long as it is NOT mean-spirited and demeaning. We're here to learn how to be funny without hurting others. We will avoid jokes that stereotype people (for example, no dumb blonde jokes), that put people down for something that is not in their control (weight, age, ethnicity, gender, sexual identity, etc.), or that are mean for the sake of being mean. We can choose to be funny in many ways that don't hurt people's feelings.

(cont'd.)

3. **No profanity.** You can't shock me; I've heard it all. But we're trying to be *funny*, and cursing is so, well, *ordinary*. Maybe while we're at it, we can improve our vocabulary!

4. **If something makes you uncomfortable, speak up.** We don't know something's bothering you unless you let us know.

5. **The best comedy involves you.** If you, as the comedian, are at the center of the joke, fewer people will be offended. This does not mean you'll be putting yourself down. It means focusing the laughs on issues that personally involve you.

Key to the Icons
Used in the Games

To help you find games suitable for a particular situation, the games included in this book are coded with symbols or icons. These icons tell you, at a glance, the following details about the game:

- the recommended age of the participants
- the size of the group needed
- if a large space is needed
- if physical contact is or might be involved
- if props are required

These icons are explained in more detail below.

The recommended age of the participants. Each game belongs in a different age-group category, but in practice many of the games for younger players are also suitable for older children. Many of the games also are adaptable and can be made to suit a different age group. A minimum age recommendation is given for each game, using this icon:

 = young children (7 to 9 years old)

 = older children and teens (10 to 16 years old)

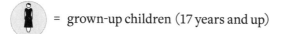 = grown-up children (17 years and up)

= children of all ages (7 years and up)

The size of the group needed. This book includes games for groups of all sizes, from individuals to large teams. If a game requires a large number of players or groups of a specific size, the game will be marked with the appropriate icon:

 = The whole group works together.

 = Players work individually, so any size group can play.

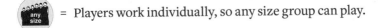 = Players work in small groups.

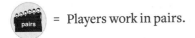 = Players work in pairs.

If a large space is needed. A large space is required for a few of the games, such as when the whole group is required to form a circle or to walk around the room. These games are marked with the following icon:

 = The game may require a larger space.

If physical contact is or might be involved. Although a certain amount of body contact might be acceptable in certain environments, the following icon has been inserted at the top of any games that definitely involve contact or might involve anything from a small amount of contact to minor collisions. You can figure out in advance if the game is suitable for your participants and/ or environment.

 = Physical contact is involved or likely.

If props are required. Many of the games require no special props. In some cases, though, items such as costumes, whiteboards, chalkboards, or other materials are integral to playing a game. Games requiring props are flagged with the icon below, and the necessary materials are listed under the Props heading.

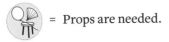 = Props are needed.

Note: Throughout this book, pronouns switch between *she* and *he*—rather than using "he/she"—to avoid clunkiness in writing. Yes, even comedy writers aspire to be grammatically correct!

The Games

Finding Your Inner Funny

Cracking the Ice

Comedians want to crack people up, so the games in this section are designed to help players become comfortable with each other while bringing smiles and giggles to everyone in the room. These are good go-to games when you're meeting with a new group of kids or grown-up kids and trying to help them relax and let their inner self out.

1   What's Funny About Me

This game helps players get to know each other's names and a little bit more while simultaneously encouraging them to explore their natural comedic talents. (Yes, we all have them.)

Directions Introduce this game by letting all of the players know that everyone has some special funny talent. For example, some people can whistle with their noses or make their eyebrows move one at a time. In this game, each player will introduce himself, describe one of his funny skills, and then demonstrate it.

Tips

- If a player can't think of anything, prompt him with suggestions.
- Once everyone has had an opportunity to contribute, chances are some of the players will think of a second thing they can do that is funny. If so, allow everyone to demonstrate a second funny talent.

Variation Each player performs a funny talent, and then everyone else in the group attempts the same thing.

2 Hello! And You Are…?

Introducing yourself to people you don't know can be awkward and especially difficult for anyone who is a little shy. This game allows the players to introduce someone they don't know but do so by describing themselves. The laughs come from incongruity.

Directions Ask the players to pair up. (Encourage opposite sex pairings or older/younger pairings because this creates incongruity, which makes things funnier.) The pairs will stand in front of the rest of the group as they give their introductions.

© Photodisc/Thinkstock

Suggest that each player tell the group about herself, but to do so by pretending to introduce her partner. For example, let's say that players Heather and Josh are paired up. Heather might introduce Josh by saying: *"This is Josh, and he loves the* Twilight *movies and going to the mall with his friends on the weekend. His least favorite subjects in school are math and P.E. He loves dressing up his cat in crazy outfits."*

Josh might introduce Heather with: *"And this is Heather. She wants to be a professional baseball player or a stand-up comic. Her favorite things to do on the weekend are playing video games and training her ferret to do stupid tricks."* By allowing players to introduce each other, they may be less nervous about telling the group a little about themselves, especially once the laughter starts.

Tip Recommend that players choose at least one thing about themselves they think is probably not true for the player they're "introducing."

Variations

- Have each player introduce the person to his or her right instead of partnering.
- Do this as a ventriloquist act. One player introduces another who attempts to lip sync what is being said.
- Have the player being introduced act out the introduction as the other player makes it.

3   You Compliment Me

Many of the everyday things we laugh at aren't actually funny. When we're a little nervous, many of us tend to laugh to release tension and anxiety. This game creates laughter from nervous tension because many of us get a little flustered when giving or receiving a compliment.

Directions Seat the players in a circle, either in chairs or on the floor. Tell them that you want them to turn, one at a time, to the person to their right and give that person a heartfelt compliment and to make it very descriptive. Suggest ideas such as, "*I love your glasses. They make you look like Clark Kent. Are you secretly Superman?*" or "*You have a great laugh. When you laugh even my belly button wants to giggle along,*" but encourage them to think of their own.

Once each player has complimented the player to her right, have her turn to the left and give that new person a compliment. By the end of the game, each participant will have given and received two compliments. You will also observe a lot of laughter and may want to ask the players what it is that they laughed at. Chances are a lot of laughter came not from anyone purposely trying to be funny, but just from having fun being with and being nice to each other. This game helps you teach your players that comedy and laughter don't have to come from "making fun"; it's just as easy to laugh and feel good about one another.

Tip After the laughter dies down, let the players know that this game helps them remember that they can be funny in a positive way.

4 Faking It

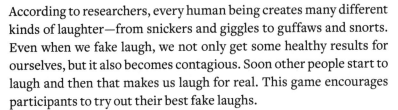

Prop A stopwatch

According to researchers, every human being creates many different kinds of laughter—from snickers and giggles to guffaws and snorts. Even when we fake laugh, we not only get some healthy results for ourselves, but it also becomes contagious. Soon other people start to laugh and then that makes us laugh for real. This game encourages participants to try out their best fake laughs.

Directions Seat the group in a circle so that everyone can see everyone else's face. Explain to the players that there are many different kinds of laughter and that everyone will get a chance to try some fake laughing. Ask each player one at a time to attempt to fake a specific kind of laugh from the lists below for a solid fifteen seconds. More advanced players can try thirty seconds.

Types of Laughs

- belly laugh—a loud low-pitched laugh that starts at the abdomen and actually hurts because it is so loud and hard
- cackle—a laugh that you might hear a witch use

- chuckle—"ha-ha-ha" or "he-he-he"
- coughing laugh—laughter that ends with wheezing and coughing
- giggle—a higher-pitched laugh that comes more from the throat and upper chest area
- hum/laugh—laughter done with the lips closed
- quiet laugh—the kind of laugh that a lady might use when she finds something funny but is embarrassed to let it show
- snort—laughing in a way that accidentally forces air out through the nose instead of your mouth

Variation Play video clips of laughs available on YouTube and ask participants to do their best to imitate these laughs. Here are some to try: donkey laugh, Dr. Evil (Mike Myers), Homer Simpson, hyena, Ricky Gervais, Santa, Sheldon Cooper, and Woody Woodpecker.

5 Funny Audition

Props Before the game, gather some writing samples that players can read out loud. These should be dry, maybe even boring writing such as a business story from the newspaper, instructions for putting together a bicycle, or an appliance warranty manual.

Comedy is as much about how something is said and done as it is about what is said or done. This game encourages players to add their own funny twists to something that wouldn't otherwise be funny at all.

Directions Players will pretend to audition for a new comedy movie and will each get an opportunity to read something for their audition. Let them know that the "monologue" is not at all amusing and that their job is to add the funny any way they can: facial expressions, gestures, body language, inflections, accents, or whatever they can think of.

Variation One player who is not reading can serve as a movie producer. After a player has read, the producer can make recommendations, such as, "Can you read that again backward?" or "Try that again—this time while standing on one leg."

6   Silly Nonhandshakes

Most Americans who meet strangers for the first time exchange handshakes. This can be socially awkward (especially for kids), and during cold and flu season, it's definitely unhealthy. This game encourages players to create their own "nonhandshake" as a way to warm them up to the idea of using their bodies in a playful way to create comedy.

Directions Form groups of four to eight players. Ask each group to create its own funny "nonhandshake" with eight to ten different moves that can involve any part of the body doing anything. The only rule is that hands can't shake. With large groups, have each member contribute an idea; with smaller groups, have each member contribute two ideas.

The groups should make up their "nonhandshake" and practice together until each individual knows the moves well. When everyone is ready, ask each player to find someone from another group to teach her handshake to. Then the players switch, and the teacher becomes the student and learns the other handshake.

Tips

- The sillier the moves, the more fun the game will be.
- Using legs and feet always spices up the movements.

Variations

- Each group demonstrates its handshake for everyone.
- Ask that each person include a noise that goes along with his or her contribution to the "nonhandshake."

7   Voice-Overs

Prop A television large enough for everyone to see it simultaneously

An easy way to create laughter from misdirection is to put the words in someone else's mouth. This game does just that.

Directions Tune a television to any nonviolent program (animal shows, sitcoms, and how-to shows all work really well, as do infomercials) and mute the volume. Select the same number of players for the game as there are people (or animals) on the screen.

Ask each player to voice one character. Although you want the players to try to be funny, encourage the group to create a story line that flows from person to person rather than just throwing out funny lines. Once you feel they've gotten as much from the game as possible, switch channels and invite another group to play.

Tip Funny accents help make this game even more fun.

Variations

- Add an extra player who is in charge of sound effects and music. Sound effects may be made using any items available in the room.

- Encourage any from the group who are not actively involved in the game to serve as the "laugh track." Suggest they laugh hard and obnoxiously.

8 Follow the Body Part

This game is designed to get players thinking about how to use their bodies for comedic purposes. You might want to read a list of body parts for the players to choose from (one is provided below) to avoid having preteens and teens immediately gravitate to sexual body parts.

Directions Ask every player to choose a different body part (if the group is large, you may have more than one player per body part). External parts are easier, but the players may choose anything on or in the body. Do not tell them what they will be doing with the selected body part (this adds to the humor of the game).

Body Parts List

ankle	ear	hand	liver	shoulder	throat
brain	elbow	head	lung	stomach	toe
butt	eye	heart	nostril	tailbone	tongue
cheek	eyebrow	kidney	ribs	teeth	
chin	foot	knee	shin	thigh	

Once everyone has selected a body part, divide the group in two and have half of the group stand on one side of the room and the other half stand on the other side. Ask one player from one side to cross the room, letting her chosen body part lead the rest of her body. For example, if Samantha chooses "tailbone," she might back across the room, perhaps bent over the entire way. The next player from the opposite team then takes a turn. This goes on until the members of both teams have crossed to the other side, one at a time.

Tip A heart moves differently than a nostril, not only in speed, but what happens while crossing the room (a heart may pulsate, while a nostril may sniff for an extended period of time).

Variations

- Have the players dance, with their body part in the lead.
- Incorporate this idea into a simple scene, with the body parts talking as well as doing physical action.

9   Fractured Clichés

Props   Collect clichés, type them out in a large font (don't capital-ize the first word), print them out, and then cut them in half. For example, with "you can lead a horse to water, but you can't make him drink," you'd have two pieces: "you can lead a horse to water," and "but you can't make him drink." You'll find a sample of fractured clichés to use at the end of this section. Feel free to use those and add others to the mix.

Writing is usually something we do by ourselves, but because we laugh more when we share our activities with others, this writing game is done in groups. It's a great way to get groups comfortable working together and understanding each other's sense of humor in the process.

Directions   Seat groups of four to six players around round tables or on the floor so that the players can all work together easily. Distribute at least fifty different fractured clichés randomly (mix them up thoroughly beforehand) to each group of players. Ask the players to work together to combine the clichés in a way that yields new and funny sayings. Let them know that if they need to add small words such as *the, and,* or *because,* they may do so.

Clichés

either lead, follow, or	*get out of the way*
those who can't do	*teach*
if you can't stand the heat,	*get out of the kitchen*
don't burn your	*bridges*
the apple doesn't	*fall far from the tree*
every cloud has a	*silver lining*
go with	*the flow*
if it ain't broke,	*don't fix it*
if you can't beat 'em,	*join 'em*
what goes around,	*comes around*
think outside	*the box*
the purpose of life	*is to be happy*
six of one;	*half a dozen of the other*
dog and	*pony show*
if at first you don't succeed,	*try, try again*
never let them see you	*sweat*
in case of emergency,	*break glass*

(cont'd.)

you had me at	*"hello"*
I'll get you	*and your little dog, too*
now we're	*cooking*
crazy like	*a fox*
money makes	*the world go 'round*
let me play	*devil's advocate*
if the shoe fits,	*wear it*
do you think I'm made	*of money?*
there's no fool	*like an old fool*
age before	*beauty*
help! I've turned into	*my mother*
his bark is worse than	*his bite*
don't judge a book	*by its cover*
it takes two	*to tango*
a woman's work	*is never done*
what's good for the goose,	*is good for the gander*
when the going gets tough,	*the tough get going*
you are my	*sunshine*
when you lie down with dogs,	*you get up with fleas*
the bigger they are,	*the harder they fall*
all dressed up and	*no place to go*
as welcome as	*a skunk at a lawn party*
blood is thicker	*than water*
liar, liar!	*pants on fire*
it takes a village	*to raise a child*
as clear as	*the nose on your face*
but, Captain,	*that would be illogical*

Once the laughter starts to die down—which is always a good clue that it's time to stop a comedy game—ask each person from a group to read his favorite new cliché aloud.

Tips

- New clichés that don't make sense can be really funny because they are incongruous.
- Sometimes three or four cliché parts can be strung together for even more fun.

Variation Rather than creating new clichés, have the groups write a story using as many of the listed clichés as possible, adding other words where necessary.

10 Words Are Funny

Props Funny words (listed below), which you have typed out and cut apart so that each word is separate from the others

People who have studied what makes us laugh have identified certain words that tend to tap into our funny bone, especially when those words are thrown *namby pamby* into a sentence. (See how that worked?) This game encourages players to explore the use of funny words with which they may or may not be familiar.

Directions Hand out two or three funny words to each player. Let players know that they do not have to know what the words mean; in fact, it's usually funnier if they don't. Ask two players to stand up in front of the group and have a conversation with each other about the day each has had. Tell the players to toss each of their funny words into the conversation as many times as they can.

Funny Words

bamboozled	coot	hornswaggle
bazinga	didgeridoo	hullabaloo
bevy	dingy	indubitably
bifurcate	doodle	janky
bilirubin	doohickey	kabob
bobolink	emu	kahuna
buccaneer	eschew	katydid
bulgur	fiddle dee-dee	kerplunk
bumfuzzle	finagle	kinkajou
cankles	flanker	knickers
canoodle	flux capacitor	lackadaisical
cantankerous	gobsmacked	loopy
carbuncle	grog	mugwump
caterwaul	grunion	namby pamby
cattywampus	gumption	noggin
cheeky monkey	gunky	pantaloons
chimichanga	hitherto	passel
conniption	hoi polloi	persnickety

(cont'd.)

popinjay	snuffle	wasabi
prestidigitation	spelunker	weasel
proctor	spork	wenis
rapscallion	sprocket	whatnot
rookery	squeegee	wombat
rumpus	tater	wonky
scotch	tookus	zamboni
scurvy	tuber	zazzy
scuttlebutt	viper	zippity
smorgasbord	waddle	
snarky	walkabout	

Tips

- Players may pronounce words in any way they want.
- In this game, stumbling over the words works to a player's advantage.

Variations

- All the players make up definitions for the funny words.
- Each participant acts out what she thinks her funny word means.

Let's Get Physical

One of the reasons that younger kids laugh so much more than teens and grown-ups is that young children know more about using their bodies to play. Ask yourself how many thirty-year-olds you see playing on monkey bars or skateboarding to work, and you'll see what I mean. Grown-ups consider their bodies transportation for their brains—and that's no fun at all.

The games in this section may be much easier for younger kids to jump right into than they are for teens or adults to embrace. But to maximize the laughs, it's important that everyone learn to use his or her body in the silliest ways possible. In fact, by engaging our bodies in trying to be funny, we engage muscle memories, where the fun of our youth is stored.

11 Funny Faces

Words can be funny, but sometimes it's how our faces look while we're talking that makes people laugh. In fact, even without saying a word, a face can create comedy all on its own.

Directions Ask two players to compete with each other to perform the funniest facial expression from the list below (or add your own). Ask them not to talk, use other body parts, or add noises; this game is all about letting their faces do all the work. Suggest they not just "do the face" but also milk it for all the laughs they can get.

List of Funny Faces
You are:

- feeling ashamed
- eating something horrible
- trying to shoo a bee off your nose
- bored out of your mind
- trying to register emotions but you've just had Botox injections
- unable to see without squinting
- winking uncontrollably/unable to stop winking
- in pain—a car just ran over your foot
- a cat with a hairball
- a chipmunk with cheeks full of nuts
- constipated
- practicing your Elvis lip
- not in control of your eyebrows
- making a fish face
- flirting
- finding out you're pregnant
- just learning to smile
- trying to talk after your lips have disappeared
- trying to ignore an itchy nose
- working with a Novocaine mouth

- seeing a large bear coming toward you
- practicing a soap opera mystery face
- smelling something tasty
- tasting something sour
- trying not to sneeze
- watching a fly circle the room

Tips

- Players who repeat a funny face a few times have more fun and get better at it.
- Moving faces are funnier than static ones.

Variations

- Snap a picture of each funny face so that players get a chance to see what they look like.
- Have a face-off, with each winner taking on the winner of the next funny-face competition. In the end, the rest of the group members vote for their favorite funny face.

12 Stuck on You

Many comedy games, especially improv and sketch comedy, require players to be comfortable touching each other. This game helps players understand that in the context of these games, touch can be used for comedic effect. For teenagers, you may want to establish boundaries, pair players of the same gender, or encourage volunteers rather than selecting players at random.

Directions In this game, players pretend to be glued to each other and must play out a scene without separating. Appropriate body parts at which the players may be joined include: arms, shoulders, hands, elbows, feet, legs, hips, or heads. Players not in the scene should suggest actions for the "stuck" players to try to accomplish together. Here are some ideas to prime the pump: try on hats, wash windows, ride a bike, dance a jig, or hitchhike.

Tips

- If each player approaches the task differently, the humor stakes rise.
- Bigger movements are funnier than smaller ones.

Variations

- Try the game with three players glued together.
- At the end of each scene, the players must devise a way to get unstuck that is as funny as possible.

13 Duck, Duck, Moose

Every young American child or anyone who was ever a child is probably familiar with the game Duck, Duck, Goose. This game puts a comedic spin on a classic by letting kids race around the circle as a variety of animals.

Directions Seat players in a circle, making sure to have enough room around the outer edges of the circle for running and play. Explain to the group that this game is exactly like Duck, Duck, Goose with one exception. The person who is "it" will go around the circle tapping everyone's head and saying "duck" until he has chosen someone to be "it." Instead of calling "goose," the first player will call out any animal's name he wants, for example, moose. The player who has been chosen as the moose must now act like a moose as he chases the first player around the circle, racing back to the spot where they started. Whoever makes it back to the spot first takes a seat, and the player still standing is now "it." The game continues until everyone has had a chance to play.

Tips

- Animal sounds make this game more exciting.
- Not all animals move in the same ways. For instance, a sloth does not run in the same way as a cougar does.

Variation The two players are both animals. The chooser retains his animal character as he names the animal for the seated player.

14   Silly Shambles

Even the simple act of crossing a room can be filled with comedy if the players involved use their imaginations. This game encourages players to realize that even simple everyday physical actions can be made funny.

Directions   Invite one player at a time to cross the room in the silliest way she can imagine. Examples of funny ways of crossing a room are listed below; use these ideas to get the group to start thinking of their own ideas. As one player walks the room, the rest of the players watch so that when it is their turn, they do not repeat the same moves when each of them takes a turn.

Funny Ways to Cross a Room

doing bad cartwheels	rolling downhill
being chased by bees	rowing a boat
fire walking	scooching
flirty walking	moving in a serpentine way
struggling with gum on a shoe	stomping
hanging from a helicopter	swimming
moving like a hovercraft	stilt-walking
ice-skating	stumbling
jungle vine-swinging	tiptoeing
walking with knees glued together	walking like a mermaid
pogo sticking	walking in flippers
roller-skating out of control	walking on the moon

Variations

- Two players play, with one crossing in a silly manner and another attempting to repeat the same moves.
- Audience members yell out "Faster" or "Slower," and the players speed up or slow down.

15   Body Switch

Some of the funniest movie comedies are those in which people are in the wrong body, for example, *Freaky Friday, Big, 13 Going on 30,* and *All of Me.* The game Body Switch allows players to create laughter from imagining what it would be like to be stuck in someone else's body for a while.

Directions   This game relies heavily on the incongruity of the person and the new body she inhabits. The idea is that each player is actually someone else completely different, and she has, for some reason, ended up in the wrong body. A female player may "actually" be a professional basketball player, a weight lifter, or an octogenarian, for example.

Choose two players. Ask the rest of the group to suggest ideas for an odd person who one of the players has trapped inside him or her; the other player will be "normal." Also ask the group for a scene for the two to act out.

Tips

- A new body is like a new car; at first, it will be hard to operate.
- Exaggerated movements are funny. How would the strange body walk, gesture, or sit, for example?

Variations

- The person inside can be a famous persons such as Elvis Presley or Lady Gaga.
- Instead of a person, imagine that what's inside is an animal or an alien.

16 Mirroring

Trying to do the exact moves as someone else as quickly as he does them is a comedy technique rife with comedy. If you need a good example of this, watch the *I Love Lucy* episode in which Lucille Ball attempts to mirror Harpo Marx and try not to laugh.

Directions Pair players and assign one to be a person looking into a mirror and the other to be the first player's reflection. Ask the first player to do some moves he would normally do in front of a mirror. He should move slowly at first and then more quickly to make the game more challenging for player #2, who must try to mimic those moves in real time.

Tips

- Adding funny facial expressions is a good way to challenge the "mirror" player.

- Approaching and leaving "the mirror" can add a level of comedy to the game.

17 The Eyes Have It

whole group

Many famous comedians have been known for their unusual eyes or how they used them. Think of Marty Feldman, Phyllis Diller, Rodney Dangerfield, and Jim Carrey. Body language experts say that our eyes and eyebrows communicate more than all the rest of our body. This game encourages players to let their eyes and eyebrows do the talking.

Directions Choose two players for this game, one of whom will carry on a conversation using words, hand gestures, facial expressions, etc., and the other who will not say anything and have to communicate only with the upper half of her face.

Ask the rest of the players to suggest a scene in which two people would have a conversation—standing at a bus stop, going on a first date, or attending a job interview, for example. The two players will create a scene, with one doing all the talking and the other responding only with her eyes and eyebrows. The player who talks should read the eye "language" and respond as if the silent partner is actually talking.

Tips

- Eyes don't just move right and left or up and down—you can use big eyes, squinty eyes, darting eyes.... The possibilities are numerous.
- Suggest that players avoid wearing hats during this game. A hat can cast a shadow over the eyes.
- Stick-on eyebrows make this game even more fun.

Variations

- One player plays alone and is assigned up to five different emotions to communicate with his eyes.
- Use two players but ask both to communicate only with their eyes.
- Use a bandana to cover the second player's nose and mouth to make it easier for to focus only on his eyes.

18 Bigger/Smaller

Many years ago, two of my male players—one of whom was very tall and skinny and the other who was very short and paunchy—decided to dress in black unitards and just stand together on a stage, wordlessly, for several minutes. What a great way to reinforce that comedy can come simply from things that are odd and don't seem to belong together. The audience laughed the entire time the guys were on stage. Like that scene, this game plays with the concept of size, encouraging players to explore the range of funny things their bodies can express.

Directions Select two players and ask them to converse with each other about any topic. But instead of just standing there while they talk, one player will make herself as big as possible, while the other makes herself as small as she can. Encourage the players to think of all the ways in which they can become bigger (arms out to the side, standing up tall, pushing their stomachs out, etc.) or smaller (arms and legs in tight, lying on the floor, standing sideways, etc.). Midway through the game, call "Switch," at which point the players should continue the conversation but do the opposite behaviors with their bodies.

Variation Each player transforms from big to small (or small to big) in the course of the game, trying to make sure she is never the same size as the other player.

19   Funny Cheers

We're accustomed to seeing highly choreographed cheerleaders rooting on their favorite sports teams, but when a group of people is given a short amount of time to create a cheer routine for an odd event or thing, the result is often hysterical.

Directions Form groups of three to five players and give each "cheerleading squad" something unusual to create a cheer for. (See the list of ideas below to get started.) Allow each squad five minutes to put a routine together—any longer and it may be too well developed to be funny.

Odd Things to Cheer For

air	gum chewing	
ballet	flush toilets	
bicycle riding	homework	a rock concert
camping	lawn mowing	shopping
cars	the library	silence
checkers	low-fat milk	skateboarding
cheerleaders	Milky Way galaxy	skunks
a chicken crossing the road	Monday	sleeping
	mosquitoes	spaghetti
couch potatoes	paint drying	texting
dirt	pants	umbrellas
a dog show	parents	walking
a fire	recess	weekends
flies	the remote control	work

Tell players to be as creative as possible in creating a cheer for their specific event, rather than relying on something general that could be used to cheer on anyone or anything.

Tips

- Words that rhyme or can be spelled out with bodies are always fun.
- One klutzy "cheerleader" always adds comedy, whether that person is naturally clumsy or just acting.

20   Machine

Some people say that it won't be that long until all people are replaced by machines. Well, if you can't beat 'em, join 'em. Learn to act like a machine now, and maybe no one will be able to tell the difference in the future!

Directions Assign each player a machine from the list below. Encourage players to use their bodies, faces, and sound effects to become their machine. Give the group a few minutes to think about the kinds of movements and sounds their machine makes and then invite them to perform one at a time.

Machines

automatic hand dryer	elevator	oven	toaster
bicycle	escalator	pasta maker	toilet
bicycle pump	espresso machine	pizza cutter	train
bus	fan	refrigerator	treadmill
calculator	fax machine	rotary telephone	vacuum cleaner
camera	garbage disposal	sail boat	vending machine
can opener	hedge trimmers	scooter	washing machine
car alarm	helicopter	skateboard	water fountain
cell phone	ice maker	snowblower	weed eater
clock	lava lamp	snow shovel	wheel
coffee grinder	lawn mower	speakers	wheelbarrow
copy machine	leaf blower	stapler	wrecking ball
dryer	microwave	steamroller	
electric toothbrush	mixer	Swiss army knife	
		tablet computer	

Tip Most machines don't move as fluidly as humans, so starting and stopping can add comedy.

Variations

- Have two players transform into one machine—for example, two people are the beaters in a mixer.
- Use two players. One player is the machine, and the second is the product the machine produces, e.g., icemaker and ice. Remember to choose machines that actually make something for this variation.

21 Bad Exercise Instructor

A simple comedy rule: Anytime someone tries to do something badly and they succeed, it's going to be funnier than if they try to do something well and succeed. This game encourages players to get in touch with their inner bad exercise instructor; the results can be not only comedic but also aerobic!

Directions Have players stand in a circle. Make sure each player has enough room to spread his arms out full length. One player at a time will step to the middle of the circle and lead the rest of the group in a bad exercise move. The definition of "bad" is up to the individual players. The move can use little to no exercise at all (e.g., finger movements), exercise a weird body part such the epiglottis, parody a "normal" exercise such as push-ups done against another player, or a make klutzy move (e.g., falling down).

When player #1 has led all the other players through the move a few times, invite the next player to take the center and create his moves.

Tips

- Overly enthusiastic instructors up the yuks.
- Repeat exercises oddly. For example, do three on the right and fifteen on the left.

Variation Advanced groups can do the exercises cumulatively, adding each move they learn to the previous one.

22   Hop to It

In 1964 the great comedic duo of Peter Cook and Dudley Moore debuted a sketch called "One Leg Too Few" in which Moore applied for the job of Tarzan despite having only one leg. He hopped around wearing a trench coat so that the audience couldn't see his bent leg; he occasionally perched with the short leg on a chair. The humor came primarily from watching him hop—hopping is joyful, fun, and funny because it's not a traditional form of human movement. This game also uses hopping, but the hopping can be done on one or both legs.

Directions Invite two players to stand in front of the rest of the group for this game. Tell them that you and the group will give them a short scene to play out however they'd like, with the one requirement that one of the players should hop in some manner during the entire scene. Sample scenes are included in the list below. The nonhopping player may act surprised and talk about the hopping or may just ignore it altogether.

Hopping Scene Ideas for Younger Players

building a tree house
attending the first day of school
having to "tinkle"
talking to your kid/parent
playing hide-and-go-seek
roller skating

talking to your student/teacher
washing your dad's car
attending a job interview
praying in church
going to a therapy session

Hopping Scene Ideas for Older Players

building a house
trying bungee jumping for first time
buying coffee
robbing a bank

going on a first date
participating in a fun run
going to a high-school reunion
visiting a complaint department at store

When the first players are finished, change scenes and invite a second pair to approach their scene and the hopping in a completely different manner.

Tip Younger players have a much easier time of hopping than older players do. Keep scenes short for anyone older than twelve.

Variations

- The "hopper" doesn't do it continually but, rather, randomly and at unexpected times.
- Both players hop off and on during the game.

23　Stuck In...

We've all been stuck in something—a sweater, a boring class, a drag-on's den (okay, maybe that last one is a stretch)—and although it's probably not funny when it happens to us, reliving that experience or a similar one can evoke all kinds of laughter. The best part of this game is that it allows players to come up with creative solutions for getting unstuck...solutions that may not work in real life.

Directions Ask two players to act out a scene in which they will be stuck together in a place or situation. (The list below provides ideas to jumpstart your players' imaginations.) Encourage them to use creative approaches to get out of their predicament. For example, instead of using a hammer to get out of a box, they could blow the box apart with their bad breath.

Places and Situations to Be Stuck In

a basketball net	the principal's office
the belly of a whale	quicksand
a boring meeting at work	a roller coaster
a tiny car	the roof
a chair meant for smaller people	a seat belt
the circus fun house	a spider's web
the dryer	a straight jacket
duct tape	the toilet
a fire hydrant	a tree
a giant pill bottle	a tuba case
a life raft	a turtleneck
a pair of pantyhose	the vending machine
an old phone booth	a volcano

Tip If one player is scared of the predicament and the other is really calm, additional laughs will arise from the differences in the way they react.

Variations

- Try using three players, with two stuck and another who has to be coached to help get them unstuck.
- Just as the players seem to be on their way out of the predicament, members of the audience yell out a twist that makes the situation even more precarious.

24   So You Think You Can't Dance

Millions of people tune into dancing shows such as *Dancing with the Stars* each week. Although some viewers are undoubtedly dance fans, probably just as many are watching for the humor of watching people who dance poorly, especially in the early rounds. It isn't a coincidence that the show's producers almost always include one or two comedians and someone who appears too old or out of shape for the program. They're counting on fans sticking around through the first shows because of the humor factor.

Rather than be embarrassed by our inabilities, comedy allows us to find the humor in them that others see (sometimes at our expense). This game allows players to badly choreograph a dance with the goal of intentionally making mistakes and goofing up traditional dance moves.

Directions   Create dance teams of four or five players and encourage each player to contribute several bad dance move ideas with the goal of putting together a dance that has no grace or beauty but instead makes everyone else slap his or her thighs in laughter.

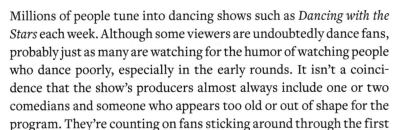

Allow dance teams five to seven minutes to choreograph a routine and then showcase each team one at a time. When a team is not dancing, its members will sit in the audience and cheer the bad moves.

Tips

- Attempts at "traditional" dance moves done poorly work well comedically.
- If all members of the dance team do the moves out of time or out of sequence, the dancers will have more fun.

Variations

- Bring in assorted costumes to inspire the choreographers.
- Give each team a dance theme such as "Lunch" or "Homework."
- Ask the rest of the players to "critique" the dance teams on technique and form.

Comedy Writing

Behind almost every form of comedy (except improv) is someone who has written the jokes, the sketches, the movie, the song, etc. Comedy writing isn't hit and miss; specific tricks and tools help writers go from "almost funny" to "laugh-out-loud funny." The games in this section help players build those skills.

Writing is often considered a solitary art—most writers conjure their magic on their own. Exceptions in the comedy world include sitcoms, televised comedy sketch shows such as *Saturday Night Live,* and comedy talk shows, all of which usually have a "stable" of "unstable" people who sit around a table, pitch ideas, and then put them onto paper. This is a much more fun way to write comedy because it encourages everyone to have a good time while being creative and sharing ideas. In this section, most of the games involve group writing so that while trying to be funny on the page, everyone is kept engaged and motivated.

All of the games in this section are best done with players seated and facing a whiteboard, overhead projector, or flip chart on which you can write down their ideas. Seeing other player's ideas helps everyone come up with even more creative (and funny) thoughts of their own.

25 Who's That Knocking?

Props A whiteboard, chalkboard, overhead projector, or flip chart on which to write players' ideas; an appropriate writing utensil

Knock-knock jokes are often kids' favorites until they reach late elementary school. Although teens and grown-up kids are easily bored or annoyed with these types of jokes, all groups are included here because older players can teach their brothers, sisters, sons, and daughters the techniques of how to write knock-knock jokes.

Directions Let the players know that they will be learning how to write knock-knock jokes. Explain that the key to writing them is choosing a word to respond to the knock with that sounds like another word or words that are easy to start a sentence with. For example, "Alaska" sounds like "I'll ask ya" or "I'll ask a."

Write the first two lines, "Knock-knock" and "Who's there?" on the board. Pick five or so words from the list of good knock-knock words (see below) and encourage everyone to toss out ideas to complete the knock-knock joke. Write down everything the players suggest. Here's an example:

Knock-knock.
Who's there?
Alaska.
Alaska who?
Alaska cat. Maybe he knows.

Good Knock-Knock Words

Word	Sounds Like	Name	Sounds Like
A herd	I herd	Abby	A bee
Adore	A door	Amanda	A man to
Alaska	I'll ask a; I'll ask ya'	Anita	I'd need a
Argue	Are you	Annie	Any
Butter	But her	Arthur	Are there
Cashew	(a sneeze)	Augusta	A gust of
CD	See the	Barry	Bury
Coincide	Go inside	Ben	Been
Dishes	This is	Carl	Carl'll
Doughnut	Do not	Cher	Share
Gopher	Go for	Eileen	I lean
Harmony	How many	Hugo	You go

(cont'd.)

Good Knock-Knock Words (cont'd.)

Word	Sounds Like		Name	Sounds Like
Honeydew	Honey do		Juan	Want
Jester	Just her		Luke	Look
Lettuce	Let us		Dwayne	Drain
Major	May your		Ida	I'd a
Police	Please		Ike	I (next word starts w/ c)
Sarong	What's wrong		Ima	I'm (next word starts w/ a)
Statue	Is that you		Isabelle	Is a bell
Tanks	Thanks		Ivana	I wanna
Tennis	Ten is		Justin	Just in
Thermos	There must		Minnie	Many
Venice	When is		Noah	No
Water	What are		Otto	Ought to
Zombies	Some bees		Robin	Robbing
			Sadie	Say the
			Turner	Turn her
			Watson	What's on
			Wilma	Will my; Will ma
			Winnie	When he

Tip The more players who suggest ideas, the more likely that a really funny knock-knock joke will be born.

Variation Pairs of players work together to write knock-knock jokes using five to eight words from the list. They get ten minutes to write, and then everyone tells a joke or two.

26 Riddle Me This

Props A whiteboard, chalkboard, overhead projector, or flip chart on which to write players' ideas; an appropriate writing utensil

What is written backward and makes people, especially young people, laugh? A riddle! This game allows players to write riddles as a group while gaining an understanding of the process so they can write their own whenever they want.

Directions Ask the players for a topic that would be fun to write about. Let's say "worm" is suggested; write the word *worm* on the board. Tell them that "worm" is going to be the answer to their first riddle. Then ask for ways to describe a worm. You might get answers such as: lives in dirt, makes compost, is used to fish with, has no arms or legs, is cold-blooded, eats leftovers. Write all those descriptions next to the word *worm* on the board.

Explain to the group that the way riddles work is to choose vague and amusing ways of describing the answer. For example:

What has no arms or legs but can compost leftovers and go fishing? A worm!

Ask for another word and encourage all the players to contribute ideas out loud as the group works together to create its own riddle.

Tip Topics that can be described in many different ways are easiest to create riddles from.

Variation Choose a word and let players pair up to create their own riddles. Then bring the group back together so players can compare their riddles to those from other groups.

27 That's So Cliché

Props A whiteboard, chalkboard, overhead projector, or flip chart on which to write players' ideas; an appropriate writing utensil

The basic idea of a written joke is simple: The *setup* makes the listener or reader think the joke is going one way, and the *punch line* veers off in another (hopefully funny) direction. Taking an old cliché and changing it up slightly is a simple first step in comedy writing because everyone knows the setup already and it's easy to play around with changing the ending. So *voilà*, you have a joke!

Directions Choose a cliché from the list provided below or think of one on your own and write it on the board. Explain to the players that they're going to write jokes by changing the ending of clichés. Give them an example by revising an expression such as *"You can lead a horse to water, but you can't make him drink"* as *"You can lead a horse to water, but you can't get him to take a shower."*

Encourage everyone to shout out his or her ideas and try to write them all down. When the enthusiasm and ideas slow down, choose another cliché to play with.

Clichés That Work Well for This Game

- A bird in the hand is worth two in the bush.
- A penny saved is a penny earned.
- All that glitters is not gold.
- All work and no play makes Jack a dull boy.
- An apple a day keeps the doctor away.
- Every cloud has a silver lining.
- The apple doesn't fall far from the tree.
- The early bird gets the worm.
- Good things come to those who wait.
- He woke up on the wrong side of the bed.
- Laughter is the best medicine.
- Let sleeping dogs lie.
- Lie down with dogs, you get up with fleas.
- She's more fun than a barrel of monkeys.
- Two's company; three's a crowd.
- You can lead a horse to water, but you can't make him drink.

- You can't have your cake and eat it, too.
- What goes up, must come down.
- When life gives you lemons, make lemonade.
- When the going gets tough, the tough get going.

Tips

- Longer clichés are easier to work with.
- Try replacing words from the cliché with others that rhyme. For example, "A bird in the hand…" can become "A nerd in the hand…"
- Use words that start with the same letters. "It takes two to tango" could be rewritten as "It takes two to tangle up the Christmas lights."

Variations

- Use advertising slogans.
- Use nursery rhymes.
- Use well-known song titles. (Country titles are especially good for eliciting laughter.)

28 Read My Bumper

Props A whiteboard, chalkboard, overhead projector, or flip chart on which to write players' ideas; an appropriate writing utensil

We see funny bumper stickers on the backs of cars every day. They make us laugh, make us think, and maybe even change our attitude for the day. But most of us never think about the fact that someone somewhere writes these pithy sayings. This comedy writing game allows players to create their own bumper stickers using well-known examples as a template.

Directions Choose a bumper sticker template from the list below or from any bumper stickers that you can think of and write it on the board. Encourage players to suggest out loud unique and funny ways to complete the bumper sticker. Write all the suggestions on the board.

Bumper Sticker Templates:

- Ask me about my...
- Caution: Driver is...
- Celebrate...
- Driver has no...
- Friends don't let friends...
- Honk if you...
- If you can read this bumper sticker,...
- I ___, and I vote
- I...
- I do whatever...
- I'd rather be...
- If you don't like my driving...
- My child is smarter than...
- Warning: I brake for...

When the ideas slow down or stop being funny, choose another template to play with.

Tip The odder the idea, the funnier it can be. "Caution: I brake for leprechauns" gets more laughs than "Caution: I brake for Boy Scouts."

29 The Stories My Bumper Can Tell

Props A whiteboard, chalkboard, overhead projector, or flip chart on which to write players' ideas; an appropriate writing utensil

Directions Bumper stickers are also the inspiration for this game, but rather than simply filling in a blank, the players create a story based upon funny bumper stickers. (See the list below for ideas to get your players started.) Either provide a written list of the bumper stickers to each player or show the list on an overhead projector.

Funny Bumper Stickers

- 5 out of 4 people have a problem with fractions.
- Allow me to introduce myselves.
- Ambivalent? Well, yes and no.
- Beware of all enterprises that require new clothes.
- Can I trade this job for what's behind door #2?
- Clear the road! I'm 16!
- Do I look like a people person?
- Don't follow me. I'm lost, too.
- Errors have been made. Others will be blamed.
- Every time I get with the program, someone changes the channel.
- Heavily medicated for your safety.
- Help! I'm having an out-of-money experience.
- I base my fashion taste on what doesn't itch.
- I don't get even; I get odd.
- I am a deeply superficial person.
- If at first you don't succeed, destroy all evidence that you tried.
- If you can't be a good example, be a horrible warning.
- I live in my own little world, but it's okay, they know me here.
- I'm only wearing black until they make something darker.
- I started out with nothing and still have most of it left.
- I used to care, but now I take a pill for that.
- Lord, give me patience, but hurry.

(cont'd.)

Funny Bumper Stickers (cont'd.)

- My other bumper sticker is funny.
- Never trust anyone over 10.
- Out of my mind; back in five minutes.
- Plan to be spontaneous tomorrow.
- Please do not honk. Driver trying to sleep.
- This is not an abandoned vehicle.
- We regret to inform you that tomorrow has been cancelled due to lack of interest.
- What happens if you get scared half to death twice?
- Why is *abbreviation* such a long word?
- You! Off my planet!

Each player will write by herself for this game. She may write any kind of funny story she wants as long as it incorporates the bumper stickers she has been given. Here is an example you can read to help players understand the game. This one uses five bumper sticker sayings:

"Ambivalent? Well, yes and no," she said hesitantly as I fiddled with the radio dial, trying to find a station we both agreed upon.

She stared at me vacantly because she was heavily medicated for your safety, and when the patrolman drove up to the car, I smiled and said, "Hello, officer. Put it on my tab!"

He looked inside and winked. "I should ticket you because friends don't let friends drive naked, but I'm a deeply superficial person."

Allow each player no more than 10 minutes to write her story, as longer periods of time tend to drag the game down. When the time is up, ask each player to read her bumper sticker story out loud to the rest of the group.

Variations

- Players work in pairs to write their stories.
- Everyone uses the same ten bumper stickers to write a story.

30   I Am Spam; Spam I Am

Props A list of easy-to-rhyme words (see below), typed out and distributed to the players

Dr. Seuss, nursery rhymes, limericks…all are versions of poetry that tell a story while rhyming. This game helps players explore rhyme as a comedy writing tool by creating their own funny short poems and reading them aloud.

Directions This game is about writing a funny rhyming poem (not a beautiful poem, a thoughtful poem, or a deep and insightful poem). Each player will have five minutes to compose a poem using any of the rhyming words from the list below and then read hers out loud to the group.

Easy Rhyming Words

- air, bear, care, chair, dare, fair, glare, hair, lair, mare, pear, rare, scare, share, spare, stare, tear, there, wear

- all, ball, brawl, call, crawl, doll, fall, gall, hall, loll, mall, shawl, sprawl, tall, wall

- back, black, clack, crack, hack, knack, lack, pack, quack, rack, sack, slack, stack, track, whack

- ban, bran, can, fan, man, plan, ran, scan, span, tan, than, van

- bat, cat, chat, fat, flat, gnat, hat, mat, pat, rat, sat, scat, spat, that, vat

- bay, bray, cay, day, gray, hay, lay, may, neigh, pay, play, pray, ray, say, spray, stay, they, whey, yay

- bed, bread, dead, dread, fed, fled, head, led, read, red, said, sled, spread, wed

- bee, debris, fee, flee, flea, free, gee, key, knee, me, pea, sea, see, ski, spree, thee, tree, wee

- bet, debt, fret, get, jet, let, met, net, pet, set, sweat, threat, vet, wet, yet

- bit, fit, flit, grit, hit, kit, knit, lit, mitt, pit, quit, sit, slit, skit, spit, wit

- bite, fight, flight, fright, kite, knight, light, might, night, plight, quite, right, sight, slight, sprite, tight, white

(cont'd.)

Easy Rhyming Words (cont'd.)

- blip, chip, dip, flip, grip, hip, lip, nip, quip, rip, sip, slip, strip, tip, trip, whip, zip
- book, brook, cook, crook, hook, look, nook, rook, shook, took
- bore, core, chore, door, floor, four, ignore, lore, more, pour, roar, shore, spore, store, tore, wore, your
- bought, brought, cot, dot, fought, got, hot, jot, lot, not, ought, plot, pot, rot, slot, spot, tot, taught, thought
- brick, chick, flick, hick, kick, lick, nick, pick, quick, sick, slick, stick, thick, trick, wick
- bug, chug, dug, hug, jug, lug, mug, plug, pug, rug, slug, snug, tug, ugh
- cap, chap, clap, flap, gap, lap, map, nap, rap, scrap, slap, snap, strap, tap, trap, zap
- cry, dry, eye, fry, high, lie, my, nigh, pie, rye, shy, sigh, spy, spry, thigh

Before starting, provide an example of a funny rhyming short poem, such as:

I am wet
Exclaimed the vet
Who lost the bet
To a golden retriever he'd never met.
And yet,
he didn't fret
or even get
a beach towel or a blow dryer set
to "slightly less than wet."

If your group of players includes younger kids and either teens or grown-up kids, remind players to keep their poetry clean.

Tips

- Unlike real poetry, the less thinking the players do the better.
- A good way to start is to pick one word that seems funny from the list of rhyming words and create from there.

Variations

- Assign each player a different group of rhyming words.
- Have two players team up to write a shared poem.

31 The Group Poetry Society

Props A list of easy rhyming words (from Game #30), typed out and distributed to players

Using the funny rhyming technique from the last game, this game proves that poetry + mystery = comedy.

Directions Use the same rhyming words from Game #30 ("I Am Spam; Spam I Am") to help make this an easier and more-fun activity for everyone. Assign one word ending to each player; for example, player #1 has words ending in "ack," player #2 has words ending in "ook," etc. Each player will write the opening line of his poem, ending in a rhyming word from his list, at the top of a clean piece of paper. After about twenty seconds, call out "Pass," and all of the players will pass their paper to the player on their right.

Each player must write a new line that rhymes with the one on the page now in front of him. After twenty seconds, call "Pass" again and the process continues. Do this until everyone has worked on every poem at least once; it is okay for players to repeat a rhyming word. Let players know when they are working on the last line so that they can tie things up.

Ask each player to read the poem he that he began.

Tips

- Short lines are easier than long ones.
- Poems that tell a story make this game more fun for everyone.

32 Weird Holidays, Weird Cards

Props A whiteboard, chalkboard, overhead projector, or flip chart on which to write players' ideas; an appropriate writing utensil

Why limit yourself to only the greeting cards available online and in stores? And what about the many holidays that don't have cards of their own? This game encourages players to use their sense of humor to create weird and funny cards for weird and funny holidays.

Directions Ask if there are any players who think they can draw funny images and assign those as the team captains for groups of two to four players. Let the teams know that they will get to write and draw funny greeting cards for odd holidays. (A partial list is included below.)

Choose a different weird holiday for each team and allow each team ten minutes to create as many funny cards as they can. When the time is up, have teams show and read their cards aloud.

Odd Holidays (Real and Imaginary)

- Annoy Your Sister Day
- Bathe Your Cat Day
- Dress Up Your Pet Day
- Eat Your Vegetables Day
- Extraterrestrial Abductions Day
- Eyebrow Awareness Day
- Facebook Stalkers Day
- Festival of Sleep Day
- Fortune Cookie Day
- Groundhog Day
- Hoarders Day
- Honesty Day
- Houseplant Appreciation Day
- Juggling Day

- Loose Tooth Day
- Middle Child's Day
- National Hat Day
- National Hugging Day
- No Cellphone Day
- No Housework Day
- No Socks Day
- Panic Day
- Pretend to Be Someone Else Day
- Procrastination Day
- Roll Your Eyes at Someone Twice Your Age Day
- Scared of Something Day
- Second Cousin Once Removed Day
- Squirrel Appreciation Day
- Take Your Penguin to Work Day
- Tap Dance Day
- Tell a Lie Day
- Therapy Day
- Waffle Day

Tips

- If a team wants to use rhymes, the list of Easy Rhyming Words from Game #30 will help.
- To avoid wasting paper, teams may write their "cards" on the whiteboard or chalkboard.

Variations

- Give each team the same five weird holidays to write cards for.
- Instead of teams, write funny greeting cards together as a large group and then let everyone provide an illustration.

33 Then This Happened...

Props A whiteboard, chalkboard, overhead projector, or flip chart on which to write players' ideas; an appropriate writing utensil

This comedy writing game is similar to the old party favorite Mad Libs, except that the players can fill in any words (not limited by parts of speech or having to know parts of speech). The end goal is to create a silly headline that might be read on the front page of a tabloid paper.

Directions Write one of the partial headlines from the list below on the board and encourage everyone to suggest as many funny ideas for filling in the blanks as they can. Remind the players that odd and unexpected examples usually end up creating the most laughter. For example, "Coffee Causes People to Dress in Mohair" is funnier than "Coffee Causes Headaches."

Funny Headline Fill-in-the-Blanks

_____ About to Take over the _____

_____ Adopts _____

_____ Caught _____

_____ Causes _____

_____ Discovered to Cure _____

_____ Emerges from _____

_____ Found in _____

_____ Grows in _____

_____ Leaves Fortune to _____

_____ Pregnant with _____

_____ Really Exists! _____

_____'s Secret Revealed: _____ Is Really _____

_____ Sings _____

Talking _____ Says _____

Variations

- Ask players to fill in headlines with words beginning with a specific letter.
- Suggest players fill in the blanks with funny words from the list in Game #10, Words Are Funny.

34 Rent My Room/ Don't Get Personal

At one time or another, most of us have read or written a classified ad. Many are unintentionally funny; this game allows younger players to write a silly ad trying to rent out their bedroom while older players can create personal ads that are meant to evoke laughter, not to find a date or a mate.

Directions Tell the players they will have five minutes to write the funniest ad they can think of. For younger children, suggest they think of funny ways to describe their room. Is it messy? Does it smell like pizza and socks? Do they share it with seven hamsters and a "dumb brother"? Encourage them to include all these things in their ads and to rent it out for a funny amount.

For teens and grown-up kids, remind the group that personal ads usually include some physical details about the person writing the ad and the person he is interested in meeting, as well as a list of activities he enjoys and would like to share with someone else. Let the players know that the easiest way to make this funny is to choose really quirky personal details and odd activities. Making up funny personal ad acronyms (CSF = complicated single female) or creating new meanings for existing shorthand (NS = "no snakes" instead of "no smoking"). Lists of personal ad acronyms are available online to help jumpstart the fun.

After time has expired, ask each player to read his ad to the group.

Variations

- Have younger players rent out their parents.
- Pair up older players and have them interview each other and then write a funny personal ad for each other.

35 Funny Fortune Cookies

Props A whiteboard, chalkboard, overhead projector, or flip chart on which to write players' ideas; an appropriate writing utensil

Fortune cookie sayings can be wise, provocative, amusing, or laugh-out-loud funny. Sometimes they're a combination of all of those things wrapped up in about a dozen words and some sweet, crunchy pastry. This game encourages players to use their creativity to come up with funny prognostications about the future.

Directions Start the game by writing a few sample funny fortune cookie sayings on the board—for example, "Someone will invite you to a karaoke party," "A visit to the restroom lies ahead," and "Ignore previous fortune cookie predictions." Give players five minutes to write as many funny fortunes as they can.

When the time is up, ask each player to read hers aloud.

Tips

- Fortunes that predict doom and gloom have to be funnier than those that predict good things happening in order to get a laugh.

- If providing winning lottery numbers, make them unusual numbers such as "–3."

Variations

- Prompts such as "You will _____," "You will meet _____," and "_____ lies around the next corner" can help players get started.

- Give the players a theme for which to write fortunes—birthdays, anniversaries, graduations, or bachelorette parties all work well.

36 It Was So Funny....
How Funny Was It?

Props A whiteboard, chalkboard, overhead projector, or flip chart on which to write players' ideas; an appropriate writing utensil

One of the key elements to comedy writing is exaggeration. Exaggeration helps something go from amusing to "rolling on the floor laughing" funny. It also lets us laugh at things that might otherwise cause negative emotions such as frustration or embarrassment.

Directions Ask players for topics such as school, work, or weather. Let's say, the topic chosen is weather. Ask the players for adjectives that they might use to describe weather: *cold, hot, rainy, muggy, snowy, so windy that cars are flying through the air like cicadas,* etc. From the list, choose one adjective, for example, *cold*. Then write the sentence, "The weather was so cold _____" on the board.

Encourage each player to suggest a funny idea out loud to fill in the rest of the sentence. If the group needs a prompt, contribute your own. In this case, you might write, "I was glad to have extra hair in my ears."

Once every player has contributed an idea or two or when funny new responses are no longer being volunteered, move on to another adjective.

Tips

- Use the words *so* or *such*, as in "It was so cold..." or "He was such a penny pincher..." to help players think of exaggerations.

- To determine whether enough exaggeration is used, ask the question, "Is it likely to have happened that way?" If something might have occurred the way the joke is written, that joke needs more exaggeration.

Variation Play this more as an improv game, by lining players up in two lines that face each other. One player completes an exaggeration such as, "The thunder was so loud..." and moves to the back of his line. The player facing him completes the same sentence with a different exaggeration and then moves to the back of his line. The game continues until no one can think of anything new and funny to add.

37 Word Up

Props A whiteboard, chalkboard, overhead projector, or flip chart on which to write players' ideas; an appropriate writing utensil

As with the icebreaker game Words Are Funny (Game #10), this game relies on the inherently humorous way that certain words sound.

Directions For teens and grown-up kids, write the words from the Funny Words list from Game #10 on the board or use an overhead projector to share the list with the players. For younger kids, use the list that follows instead because it includes funny words that are more commonly used by younger children. Let the players know that they will have five minutes to write a funny story that uses as many of the words as possible.

Once time is up, ask each player to read his story.

Funny Kids' Words

aardvark	Chihuahua	gizzard	pickle	tickle
aquarium	circus	goose	pirate	troll
badger	clam	haircut	poodle	toilet
banana	cow	icicle	poopy	twisted
booger	creepy	jellyfish	popsicle	tush
boring	crunchy	joke	rutabaga	underpants
bossy	elbow	kitty	scooter	weasel
brother	electric	lazy	shocking	weird
bubble	evil	monkey	sister	wiener dog
cactus	frog	naughty	sleepy	wizard
cafeteria	funny	pants	snot	zebra
cheese	giggle	parakeet	sock	
chicken	giraffe	parents	square	

Variations

- Assign ten different words to each player and then proceed as described above.

- Assign the same ten words to two players so they can compare their stories afterward.

38 Why Ask "Why"?

Props A whiteboard, chalkboard, overhead projector, or flip chart on which to write players' ideas; an appropriate writing utensil

It's true that kids often say the darnedest things, but just as often, they ask the darnedest questions. This game should be a natural for anyone who has either been four years old or remembers what it's like to have a child that age. It relies on that one word that seems to start most sentences uttered by kids of that age: Why?

Directions Ask players to think of "Why" questions that a four-year-old might ask. Give the players prompts such as:

- "Why do people sleep?"
- "Why don't people have tails?"
- "Why does it rain?"
- "Why are some people tall and others short?"

Write four or five "Why" questions on the board or on the projector's sheet with enough space below each for possible funny answers. Encourage players to shout out unusual, odd, and funny answers for each question. Remind them to make sure their answers would be easily understood by a child. (For best results, the answers should be worded simply and not be too lengthy.)

Tips

- Speaking like a four-year-old when playing this game can help everyone get into the proper mindset.
- A short list of things four-year-olds do, scribbled on the side of the board, makes this game easier.

Variations

- Assign pairs of players one question each and have each pair write out ten answers to their question and then read their favorites aloud.
- Try the same game with "How?" instead of "Why?"
- If your group is all teens or grown-up kids, ask and answer more complicated questions but maintain the goal of making the answers as funny as possible. "Why is my bag always the last one on the carousel at the airport?" "How did I get these crows' feet?" "Why are they called crows' feet?"

39   What Does Webster Know?

Props   A whiteboard, chalkboard, overhead projector, or flip chart on which to write players' ideas; an appropriate writing utensil

As soon as kids are old enough to understand the basics of language (starting around age five), jokes based on wordplay become popular. These types of jokes continue to evoke laughter in all age groups. In fact, one of the most brilliant minds of all time, George Carlin, was fascinated by language and how comedic it can be. Here are just a few examples of his word-based jokes:

- If a pig loses its voice, is it disgruntled?
- Is a vegetarian permitted to eat animal crackers?
- Electricity is just really organized lightning.

Directions   This game encourages players to create their own unique and funny definitions to words. Unlike the board game, Balderdash, which relies on words that very few people have ever used or heard of, this game—"What Does Webster Know?"—relies on everyday words that everyone is familiar with.

Ask players for a topic that makes them feel confused. You may get answers such as: women, men, adults, kids, math, or technology. Take a vote on which topic the group would like to work from and write that on the board. Let's say you select "technology." Once you've written the word on the board, ask for words related to your topic. In this case, the list might include: fax, iPod, tablet, QWERTY keyboard, smartphone, and Android.

Choose one word at a time and ask the players to suggest alternative definitions for each that are funny but still have an element of truth to them. For example:

Smartphone—

- An expensive way to reduce your IQ.
- A device that allows you to annoy more people at the same time.

- A phone that knows more than you do and taunts you about it.
- A device that screws up your relationships faster than you ever could.
- Now that tingle you feel when you meet someone new could just be a text message.

When the ideas peter out, move on to the next word. Keep in mind that some words will generate lots of funny ideas, while others will be duds. When you come upon a dud, just move on.

Tip Younger players will have more fun with words that they already understand than with words you have to explain to them.

Variation Use abbreviations instead of words. IRS, FBI, PMS, SPCA, etc. are all examples. In this version of the game, players choose definitions that match the letters. Instead of Internal Revenue Service, you may get "income reported sporadically."

40 You Ought to Have a Motto

Props A whiteboard, chalkboard, overhead projector, or flip chart on which to write players' ideas; an appropriate writing utensil

Companies, cities, nonprofit organizations, football teams, scouting groups...all kinds of groups have mottoes that let people know what they're all about. Nike has "Just do it." Sony Playstation has "Live in your world. Play in ours." The city of Austin, Texas, goes with "Keep Austin weird." This game lets players write funny mottos of their own.

Directions Ask players for an idea for (1) a television show, (2) a group people belong to, (3) a place people regularly go, and (4) a company most people are familiar with. Write down one or two examples suggested by the players and let the group know that the game is to try to create funny mottos for each. Give this example: If we were writing a motto for the high-school cafeteria, we might write "Meatloaf every day" or "Hairnets for everyone!"

Encourage each player to contribute motto ideas for each category. When the fun dies down, the game is over.

Variations

- Form teams of two or three players and ask them to come up with their own mottos for the groups you've written on the board. Then have each team share and compare.

- Set parameters for the mottos. For example: They should be six words or less. They should rhyme.

41 Insert Caption Here

Props A collection of one-panel comic strips from your local newspaper or printed from the Internet. Good examples of one-panel strips include *Bizarro, Rubes,* or *The Far Side.* Cut out or white out the captions beforehand and bring enough different cartoons for each player in the group to have one.

Even when writing comedy, we're not limited to words. Cartoonists express their sense of humor in both words and drawings. This game allows players to write their own captions for cartoons—it helps integrate the visual and the language parts of sense of humor.

Directions Hand one cartoon to each player. Ask her not to write on the cartoon but to use a separate piece of paper to briefly summarize the picture and then write at least one caption. Call time after one minute and have players hand their cartoon to the person on their right.

When the players have captioned all of the cartoons, hold up one and ask each player to read her caption. Then hold up the next cartoon.

Tip The caption can explain what's going on in the drawing, or it can fill in words for one of the characters.

Variations

- Display one cartoon at a time on a document camera and have the group contribute ideas out loud.

- After finishing the game, ask players to draw and caption their own cartoons. When they are finished, have them share their work with the other players.

42 Five-Word Funny

In this world of texts and tweets, the ability to write short-form comedy is a bonus. This game encourages players to get right to the funny point.

Directions Ask players to suggest an idea for a topic of conversation that two people might have while texting or tweeting each other. Let's say that your group comes up with the topic of "what movie to see." Ask each player to write a back-and-forth conversation about choosing a movie in which each person uses only five words. Let the players know that not every line has to be funny, but that the goal is to make the overall text/tweet humorous. Here is an example:

> He: How about that adventure movie?
> She: You're enough adventure for me.
> He: You noticed that, did you?
> She: It's my turn to pick.
> He: Your movies make me cry.
> She: They're supposed to do that.
> He: My inner caveman weeps.

Give players five minutes to write their conversation and then ask them to read aloud what they've written.

Variation Let players write the same conversation with ten words per line and then compare the two conversations to see which they thought was funnier.

43 Top-Ten Reasons to Do a Top-Ten List

Props A whiteboard, chalkboard, overhead projector, or flip chart on which to write players' ideas; an appropriate writing utensil

The Top-Ten list is a staple of *The Late Show with David Letterman*, but it's been around for a long time and is a great technique for encouraging players to write multiple punch lines to the same setup (the headline).

Directions Ask the players to come up with a topic for which they'd like to create a top-ten list together. Suggest specific topics such as math or elevators instead of vague topics such as politics or education. Once the topic has been chosen, let the players know that a top-ten list has two parts: the headline and the punch lines. The game is to come up with ten punch lines for every headline.

The best way to come up with top-ten headlines is to think of phrases with the words *worst* or *least* in them. For example, if the topic is math, possible headlines might include: "people you'd least like to have teach your math class," "worst things that can happen if you fall asleep in math class," or "excuses your math teacher is least likely to believe when you fail a test."

Tips

- You don't have to have ten items in the list. Aim for ten, but the goal should be to create as many creative ideas as you can, whether that's seven or seventeen.

- If the players come up with only two ideas in the first few minutes, try a different headline.

44 "Dear Sir or Madam"

Who doesn't enjoy whining once in a while? The fun part about this game is that it encourages players to make their complaints funny instead of dwelling on the negative.

Directions Ask each player to think of something he would like to complain about today and to whom that complaint should be addressed. For example, if a young player wants to complain that today's school lunch included too many peas, such a letter could go to the cafeteria lady, the principal, or even the governor. If an older player wants to complain about the failure of her anti-aging cream, the letter could go to the chair of the cosmetic company, the scientists who promised the results, or to her mom for passing on her genes.

Give each player ten minutes to write a short and funny letter. Suggest that the comedy could come from how much they were affected by the problem, what kinds of resolution they are seeking, and what will happen if something isn't done. When time is up, have each player read her letter aloud to the group.

Tip Being overly formal and asking for something outrageous to resolve the problem can add an additional element of funny.

Variation Have each player give her letter to someone else, who has to create a funny response to the writer's complaint.

45   First Line/Last Line

Props A whiteboard, chalkboard, overhead projector, or flip chart on which to write players' ideas; an appropriate writing utensil

Directions Before the game, find an opening line from a book or article and a closing line from another. For example, Joseph Heller opens *Catch-22* with, "It was love at first sight," while Ernest Hemingway closes *The Old Man and the Sea* with, "The old man was dreaming about the lions."

Write the opening and closing lines on the board and ask players to write the opener at the top of a sheet of paper and the closer at the bottom. Then give everyone five minutes to write a funny story that fills in the blanks. When time has ended, have each player read her story.

Tips

- Words that have the "k" or hard "g" sound tend to elicit more laughter even on the page (people tend to sound things out in their heads). So name your characters Carl or Engelbert instead of Steve and Emily and have them drive Kias or Cadillacs.

- Wild adventures involving unexpected twists and characters can be really funny.

Variation For a little more challenging experience, provide a third sentence—as a middle sentence—and give players ten minutes to write their funny story.

46 Unfinished Business

This is an old party game that some people call Exquisite Corpse and others call Unknown Novelist. The humor comes from everyone working together but not knowing how what they're writing fits in with what came before.

Directions Ask players to get out a fresh piece of lined paper and to write a funny story-starting sentence at the top of the page. Also ask that the players write half of the next sentence and then fold the paper so that their original sentence is hidden from view while the half sentence still shows. Each player then hands his page to the player to his right. Everyone finishes the partial sentence, writes *another* partial sentence that makes sense to them, repeats the folding technique, and passes the page to the right.

As players reach the bottom of the page, a closing line is added, and the game is over. Everyone unfolds his page and reads the entire story aloud. Here is an example of a story that resulted from this game when played with eight-year-olds (the underlined passages are the parts of sentences filled in by other writers):

> *The dragon who eats marshmallows slept in my bed. He was as orange as the sun and <u>carried a hundred balloons</u>. The wind blew and <u>all my birthday candles went out</u>. I was sad because my mom said <u>I needed drops in my ears</u>. I ran away and joined the circus <u>with my dog, Snuffles</u>.*

And here's a story from a group of sixty-somethings:

> *I couldn't wait until the cornmeal started to bubble. All the dogs licked my face before chasing the mule, <u>who ate ice cream and danced to Bruce Springsteen's song, "Darkness on the Edge of Town."</u> It's my favorite song and always <u>makes you want to kiss a pig</u>. But I will never <u>smile at a stranger again</u>. Nothing but trouble <u>is my middle name</u>.*

Tips

- Printing helps this game; it can be difficult to read someone else's handwriting.
- Every partial sentence should include a subject and verb in order for the next player to have an easier job of being creative with the rest of the sentence.

47 Half the Script

Props A short two-person script (five pages or less) appropriate to the ages of your players. Type one copy of the script with only one of the actor's lines and the other actor's name but no lines. Reverse the process and type up a second copy. For example:

Copy 1	Copy 2
Max: What are you doing here?	*Max:*
Sue:	*Sue: I live here.*
Max: Oh, yeah, that's right.	*Max:*
Sue:	*Sue: How did you get in?*
Max: Your monkey let me in.	*Max:*

Make enough copies for each player to have one script. You can find many free scripts online. Search for comedies (although even dramatic scripts can become funny in this game).

Being clueless is a great way to create laughter, especially when everyone else is just as lost. This game has players attempting to guess what lines are missing from a script; the results can be hysterical.

Directions Give one script to each player (some players will get version 1, and some will get version 2) and give everyone five minutes to fill in the missing dialogue. Pair players so that each pair includes one player with version 1 and one player with version 2. Have each pair read first one script and then the other.

Variation For a bigger challenge, do this with a three-person script. For this variation, leave out two-thirds of the lines in each copy of the script.

48   Rewrite It Funny

Props Enough samples of everyday writing (dry material such as business forms, product directions, etc.) of approximately equal length for every player. (See the "Props" for Game #5 for other suggestions for writing samples.) Choose writing samples that are age appropriate.

Almost anything can be made funny, including instructions for building a bookcase, a dental intake form, or the nutrition information on a box of cereal. And anyone who develops the ability to find humor in these everyday items will never cease to be amused.

Directions Hand one writing sample to each player. Give the players ten minutes in which to make whatever writing they have in front of them amusing in any way possible—including doodles, added jokes, swapping out words for funnier ones, etc.

When the time is up, ask each player to read her funnier version of the original.

Variations

- Pair players and have them work together.
- Have everyone rewrite the same writing sample and then compare the ways in which different writers changed the sample to make the piece funnier.

Stand-Up Comedy

I've been doing stand-up comedy for twenty-one years, and I remember my best nights—and my worst nights—on the stage. While it can be completely intimidating to stand up on a stage by yourself, trying to make a room full of people laugh (people you usually can't see because the spotlight is too bright), when it works and they snort and guffaw, nothing feels more empowering. Stand-up comedy is a great balance between comedian and audience, so every performance is different, even when the jokes are the same.

Stand-up comedy is not just about telling the jokes you've written and practiced a hundred times. It's also about seeming spontaneous and conversational, engaging the audience in a way that makes them like you and using your body, face, and hands to reinforce the funny in your set.

This section of *101 Comedy Games for Children and Grown-Ups* will help players enjoy learning how to improve their stand-up skills before they grab a microphone at the school talent show or comedy club.

49 Entrances and Exits

When it comes to funny ways to come in and out of a room, no one did it better than Michael Richards, who played "Kramer" on *Seinfeld*. In fact, a great way to warm up players is to have them watch anything titled "Kramer's Entrances" on YouTube.

Directions Ask players to think of a unique and funny way to enter and exit a stage. You may want to give them prompts such as, "Your foot is asleep" or, "You are being chased by bees." Have each player demonstrate his entrance, say something funny about what just happened, and then exit in the same way.

Tips

- For young kids and teens, anything that involves falling down or almost falling down is usually funny.
- The more exaggerated the movement, the more laughs it will get.

Variations

- Have all of the players attempt to imitate each individual's funny entrance and exit.
- Have each player exit by doing his entrance in reverse.

50   Sound Off

Prop A microphone makes this game even more fun, but you can do it without one.

Even people who aren't good at sound effects (and most people aren't) can make funny noises. Who can't bark like a tiny dog, imitate an annoying alarm clock, or make doorbell sounds? This game encourages players to forget their words for a while and focus on the other funny noises that can come from their mouths and bodies.

Directions Ask players to stand up and encourage them to think of their own noises or choose noises from the list that you will provide for them (below). Have each player repeat her noise several times, trying to make it funnier each time.

Funny Sound Ideas

air coming out of balloon	dog barking	people kissing
alarm clock	dog sniffing	popcorn popping
balloon being inflated	donkey	scream
balloon popping	doorbell	siren
bee buzzing	door creaking	snake hissing
beverage being drunk	gargle	snore
boing	giggle	Tarzan yell
burp	gulp	telephone ring (old fashioned)
cat meowing	helicopter	thunder
cat purring	horse clop	tires screeching
cow chewing cud	hyena laugh	water dripping
cow mooing	jet taking off	wind blowing

Variations

- Give every player a sound. Once each person has performed solo, have the group create a song of sounds that they perform together.
- Have each player make the same sound, one at a time.

51 You're Quite a Character

We're all unusual in our own ways, and the more we let our inner weirdo out, the funnier things can be when we're trying to make people laugh. This game encourages players to focus on what makes them "a character."

Directions Ask players to write down the phrases "I love to...," I don't like...," and "I'm always...." Then ask them to fill in five words after each phrase. They'll end up with lists such as:

> "*I love to: ride my bike, play with my dog, drink coffee.*"

> "*I don't like: vegetables, heights, spiders.*"

> "*I'm always: smiling, itching, playing video games.*"

Once the players have their lists completed, ask them to choose one characteristic about themselves that they would like to talk about and act out, exaggerating as much as possible. A player who loves to ride her bike, for example, could do a monologue about how she rides it everywhere, including in the shower and in bed, while pretending to be riding the bike the entire time.

Tips

- The more extreme the characters seem, the funnier they are.
- Sound effects can help make this game even sillier.

Variations

- Ask players to perform two of their characteristics at the same time.
- Let players switch lists and perform a character that is out of character.

52 Impress Me

Props A microphone makes things more fun, but it isn't a requirement. You may also want to bring a computer and show a video from YouTube featuring someone doing accents and dialects. Remember to review any videos you intend to use before showing them to your group; some are rife with cursing.

Good comedy impressionists are truly talented—think of Rich Little, Jimmy Fallon, or Tina Fey. And while most of us can never truly sound like someone else, anyone can learn certain voice tricks to sound like a different person. This game encourages players to try different voices.

Directions Encourage players to take center stage one at a time and ask them to try something from the list of accents and speech habits.

Accents and Speech Habits

Accents

Australian	German	Japanese	Scottish
British	Indian	Jewish	Southern
French	Italian American	New Yorker	Russian

Try Talking Like

a baby	a rich and snobby person
a very excited girl	someone trying to sound sexy
a guy who's out of breath	someone who just got back from the dentist
a really loud guy	
an obvious liar	someone who sings everything
a mom talking to a baby	a slow talker
a strict parent	a Valley girl/dude
a redneck	a woman with slurred speech

Variations

- Everyone who wants to can try the same accent or speech habit.
- Two players have a conversation in the accent or speech habit they have chosen.

53 Court Gestures

Even when we're not playing charades or giving someone directions, most of us talk with our hands. When you're all alone on a stage, adding the extra excitement of hand and arm gestures can take a performance from amusing to laugh-out-loud funny. This game encourages players to be more aware of what their hands are doing and use them as comedy tools.

Directions Ask players to participate in this game two at a time. While facing each other, one player will either tell a funny story about something that happened in her day or perform a short bit of comedy material she has written. The other player will do only hand gestures—the bigger and more exaggerated, the better—to accompany the story or bit. When player #1 has finished, player #2 will take a seat while player #1 performs the same bit again—this time with the hand gestures that the second player created.

By the end of the game, each player will have paired up with someone new until everyone has had a chance to play the game.

Tips

- The fingers, hands, wrists, forearms, elbows, upper arms, and shoulders can all be involved in gesturing.
- Gestures sometimes work best in the pauses between jokes.
- In stand-up comedy, gestures sometimes have to be seen from far away, so over-the-top movements are best.

Variations

- Assign an individual part of the arm to player #2 and have her concentrate on using just that part for the gestures.
- Have a pair of players creating gestures, with each player adding a different gesture for the same joke. Player #1 then decides which gestures will work best for her.

54 Split Personality

Back in the days of Vaudeville, comedy duos such as George Burns and Gracie Allen were very popular, with one person playing the straight guy so that the other would appear even funnier to the audience. It is possible for one person to recreate this effect by himself—all it takes is some skill and a few comedy tricks. This game helps players learn to have a two-part conversation on stage for laughs without confusing themselves or the audience.

Directions Ask each player to think of two people in his life who sound very different from each other and usually have very different things to say. Some good examples include: mom and dad, student and teacher, child and parent, nerd and cheerleader, Sasquatch believer and skeptic, etc.

Invite one player at a time to take center stage and carry on a conversation between two people while on stage. Encourage players to help establish the characters by giving each a different vocal volume (soft to loud), pace (slow to fast), speech pattern, accent, stance (feminine, masculine, sloppy, erect, etc.), and set of gestures.

Tips

- Moving from one side of the stage to the other and turning as if to face the other "person" reinforces the idea that two different people are speaking and on stage.
- A simple prop such as a hat or a purse can add to the fun.

Variations

- Start the game with two different players and then ask one player to re-enact the scene by himself.
- Instead of having players perform a conversation between two people they know, have them create a conversation between two famous people.

55   Catchphrases

Many stand-up comedians use catchphrases throughout their sets; some build entire careers around these phrases. Jeff Foxworthy's "You might be a redneck if..." Lily Tomlin's "One ringy dingy," and Steve Martin's "Well, excuuuuuse me!" are all examples. Situation comedies use these phrases as well: For example, *Seinfeld* was famous for coining "Yada yada," "No soup for you!" and "Hello, Newman," while the show *Alice* featured "Kiss my grits" and *Saturday Night Live* introduced "We are two wild and crazy guys." This game lets players create catchphrases for each other.

Directions   Invite one player to stand up and talk off the cuff for three minutes about anything she would like, with the goal of making it as light-hearted and funny as possible. While that player is center stage, ask the other players to make a list of humorous catchphrases that help summarize either what she's talking about or how she comes across to the audience.

When the player is finished, have everyone read their catchphrases for her to choose from. She selects one and talks for another three minutes, inserting the catchphrase as often as possible. Let every player do this in turn.

Tips

- Anything from "Pass the potatoes" to "Mom always says 'No'" can be a catchphrase. The key is to keep it short and sweet—no more than five words and preferably three to four words.
- Words that start with the same letters (alliteration; as in "Pass the potatoes") can help make a catchphrase stick.

56 Save Me

Props A whiteboard, chalkboard, overhead projector, or flip chart on which to write players' ideas; an appropriate writing utensil

Whenever anyone gets up to perform, the potential exists for things to go wrong. The great part about stand-up comedy is that those little moments of failure can turn into some of the biggest laughs if the person on stage knows how to go from frustration to laughter quickly. This game allows players to create "savers"—funny ways to recover from typical problems on stage.

Directions Explain that by turning an awkward moment into a humorous one, players not only keep the laughs going but they learn how to be more confident that they can handle gaffes in public. Choose one comedy problem from the list provided below and work with the entire group of players to create ways to turn the problems into a setup for a new joke. Then move on to the next item in the list.

Comedy Problems

a baby cries

the microphone doesn't work

the microphone gives feedback

the microphone stand falls over

the people won't stop talking

a phone rings

a player before you does a similar joke

someone makes a loud noise

you are sweating like crazy

you forget everything

you forget your next joke

you get wrapped up in microphone cord

you spill water on yourself

you trip and fall

Although the entire group will contribute ideas for each problem, individual players should choose a saver that is most consistent with their personalities and material.

Tips

- Never bully the audience.
- Making it seem as if you planned the interruption or problem is often a good way to make it funny.

Variation Add your own funny problems to write savers for.

Sketch Comedy

Most students of comedy know at least one television sketch comedy show—from *The Carol Burnett Show* to *In Living Color* to *Saturday Night Live* or even *30 Rock*, the sitcom about the making of a fictional sketch comedy show called *TGS with Tracy Jordan*. Sketch comedy combines the best of comedy writing and performing, allowing everyone to create and take the stage together. This type of comedy also utilizes individual performer's unique talents and allows an entire group of funny people to write to showcase everyone's funniest aspects.

The games in this section involve both group comedy writing and performing. Although not all games require props or costumes, a prop box always comes in handy when doing sketch comedy. It's easy to collect hats, masks, costumes, and silly items of all kinds by visiting garage sales. A large plastic storage box with a lid, especially one with wheels and a handle, makes the ideal container.

57 Infomercial

Props A catalog filled with *As Seen on TV* items (you can find the catalog online)

Who hasn't laughed at late night infomercials for products that no one needs but for some reason seem inexplicably appealing when it's 2:00 AM and you can't sleep? This game takes an already-funny concept and makes it into a parody of itself to up the humor ante.

Directions Let everyone look at the catalog or provide a list of product names such as Air Curler, Chillow, Spin Mop, Temporary Hair Chalk, and Wraptastic (all real items sold on infomercials) to get an idea of the types of products for which they can create an infomercial.

Put players in groups of three to eight and give them ten minutes to create a funny new product, write a jingle, create a slogan, and write a script for the salesperson or people. If you have a prop box, the players can rummage among the items to find something that stirs their imagination. Allow another five minutes for rehearsal by the players who will be performing the infomercial. When time is up, stage the performances.

Tips

- The more ridiculous the product, the funnier the infomercial.
- Stock infomercial phrases include:
- "Operators are standing by."
- "Call now and receive two."
- "You'd think this product would sell for $19.95, but if you call immediately, we'll throw in...."

Variations

- Have teams present campaigns for existing products that focus on new uses for those products.
- Team members who aren't "on camera" can film the infomercial and play it back so the performers can laugh at themselves, too.

58 Fairy Tale Mix-Up

Props A costume and prop box with a variety of fairy tale–like items such as a princess costume, a troll wig, and some clear slippers. If you don't know the ins and outs of the fairy tales listed below, it wouldn't hurt to have a Kindle, Nook, other tablet, or a hard copy book of fairy tales available for reference.

Whenever two things that don't belong together are mixed up, hilarity can ensue. This game allows players to take characters and stories from two different fairy tales and write and perform a version never seen by any human, real or imaginary.

Directions Form groups of three to five players. Tell them that this game is about creating a new fairy tale my mixing up two existing ones. Let each group choose two fairy tales from the list below and give them ten minutes to create their new fairy tales. Remind them to write roles for all members of the group. Once all groups have written a new story, give them another five minutes to rehearse their lines. Then, it's lights, cameras, and crazy, mixed-up fairy tales.

Classic Fairy Tales

Aladdin

Beauty and the Beast

Cinderella

The Frog Prince

The Gingerbread Man

The Golden Goose

Goldilocks and the Three Bears

Hansel and Gretel

Jack and the Beanstalk
The Little Mermaid
Little Red Riding Hood
The Adventures of Pinocchio
The Princess and the Pea
Rumpelstiltskin
Sleeping Beauty

Snow White and the Seven Dwarfs
The Three Billy Goats Gruff
The Three Little Pigs
Tom Thumb
Thumbelina
The Ugly Duckling

Tips

- Updating the fairy tales by bringing them into the present can add to the fun.
- Consider telling the fairy tale from a minor character's perspective. For example, what would Snow White and the Seven Dwarfs look like from Bashful's perspective?

Variations

- Have groups begin their new fairy tales with one of the classics and end with the other. Their job is to bridge the gap.
- Instead of the groups completely mixing two fairy tales, have the players simply introduce a character from one story into the story they are working with.

59 Gone Country

Props Although not necessary, having a box of props and costumes, especially Western-themed items, can make this game more fun, especially for younger players.

Sometimes all it takes to start the funny juices flowing is a good title, and some country music songs can be counted on to provide just that. This game lets players try their comedy storytelling skills by writing sketches inspired by funny country song titles.

Directions Form groups of three players and let each choose from the list of funny country song titles below. Give them ten minutes to write a sketch with that title and ten minutes to rehearse their lines. Make sure each sketch has roles for every player. When time is up, it's time for each group to take the stage!

Funny Country Song Titles

- "Billy Broke My Heart at Walgreens, and I Cried All the Way to Sears"
- "Don't Cry on My Shoulders 'Cuz You're Rusting My Spurs"
- "Flushed from the Bathroom of Your Heart"
- "How Can I Miss You if You Won't Go Away?"
- "How Come Your Dog Don't Bite Nobody but Me?"
- "I Bought the Shoes That Just Walked out on Me"
- "I Don't Know Whether to Come Home or Go Crazy"
- "If Love Were Oil, I'd Be a Quart Low"
- "If the Phone Don't Ring, You'll Know It's Me"

- "I Just Bought a Car from the Guy That Stole My Girl, but the Car Don't Run, So I Figure We Got an Even Deal"
- "I Lost Frieda on the Freeway"
- "I'm Getting Gray from Being Blue"
- "I'm Just a Bug on the Windshield of Life"
- "I Sat Down on a Bear Trap (Just This Morning)"
- "I've Got Tears in My Ears from Lyin' on My Back in My Bed While I Cry over You"
- "I Wanna Check You for Ticks"
- "Love Me Like My Dog Does"
- "Mama, Get the Hammer; There's a Fly on Papa's Head"
- "My Wife Ran Off with My Best Friend, and I Sure Do Miss Him"
- "Peel Me a Nanner"
- "Saddle up the Stove, Ma! I'm Riding the Range Tonight"
- "She Made Toothpicks out of the Timber of My Heart"
- "She Thinks My Tractor's Sexy"
- "Take This Job and Shove It"
- "Who's Gonna Mow Your Grass?"
- "You Ain't Woman Enough to Take My Man"

Tip Because these are country songs, encouraging everyone to adopt a southern accent can be really funny.

Variation Have players write a musical instead of a sketch.

60 What Are You Doing Here?

Props A prop and costume box always makes things more fun

One of the easiest ways to set up laughs in a sketch is to put a character in the wrong time and/or place. Comedy movies such as *Back to the Future, Bill and Ted's Excellent Adventure, Galaxy Quest,* and *Kate and Leopold* all use this technique for lots of giggles.

Directions Create groups of three players and let them know they will be writing a short sketch featuring a person who is out of her element—either she is someplace she shouldn't be or in another time period. Give a few examples, such as a mermaid in Manhattan, a knight in the twenty-first century learning to text, or a ballerina in space.

Give the groups ten minutes to write their sketch and another ten minutes to rehearse their lines. Then it's time to let the stories unfold and the fun begin!

Tips

- The more incongruous the character to the scene, the funnier the sketch will be.
- It helps if the out-of-place character has an accent that doesn't fit into the scene.

61   Third Time's a Charm

In comedy, there is a "Rule of 3" that is often used to create a setup and then take the punch line in a different direction. This game allows players to learn to use the rule and create a short, funny sketch.

Directions Explain the Rule of 3 to the players using the following example: In comedy, things often happen in threes, with the third time resulting in the funny. For example, let's say a man walks past a window and looks inside. He doesn't see what he's looking for, so he moves on. A few seconds later, he returns and looks some more. Still nothing, so he walks away. He comes back once more and presses his nose up against the window, it opens, and he falls in.

Form groups of three players. Because this is a short and easy sketch, give players just two minutes to create a story that involves the Rule of 3 and another five minutes to rehearse their lines. Then have the groups take the stage one at a time and show off their funny stories.

Tips

- The first two actions shouldn't be rushed but should be played for maximum effect to build suspense.
- Each time an action is repeated, it should have a slight variation.
- Make sure the punch line is big and overexaggerated.

Variation Have each group write a story with two main characters. These characters experience two different repeated events but share the funny third. In the example used above, in between the man looking into the window, a woman could stare out and then leave. When the man falls in the third time, the woman who had been peering out can trip over him and they get tangled in the curtains.

62 Bad Museum Tour

Props A prop and costume box isn't required but does add to the fun

As the very funny *Night at the Museum* series of films has proved, even locations that are typically thought of as serious and stuffy can bring out the laughs. This sketch comedy game lets players be on their worst behavior while visiting the museum of their choice.

Directions Form groups of four to six players and allow each to select a museum from the list below. Ask them to create a funny sketch in which one player is a museum guide and the others are either people taking a tour or museum displays that are coming to life (e.g., statues, paintings, wooly mammoths, etc.). The group should decide whether the guide is good or bad at his job and what kinds of trouble will ensue.

Types of Museums

airplane	astronomy	hall of fame	natural history
American history	baseball	kids	science
ancient history	dinosaur	movie	train
art	fashion	music	wax

Allow ten minutes for the groups to write their sketches and five minutes for them to rehearse their roles (a shorter rehearsal period in this game encourages more improvisation). When the time is up, each group will show off just how much funny mischief they could cause (but don't) the next time they visit a museum.

Tips

- The more at odds the guide and tourists or exhibits are, the more potential for humor.
- When paintings, sculptures, or people come to life and claim everything that has been said about them is a lie, it just adds to the fun.

63 Who Wants to Be a Game Show Host?

Props Good things to have on hand include: Markers, poster board (cut into six or eight pieces), notecards (for questions), and a bell or buzzer. If you have a prop box with items that can be used for physical challenges, players can add more physical elements to their game shows. These types of items could include: hula hoops, balls, jump rope, yo-yos, Frisbees, etc. Players also may need to have access to the Internet to find the answers to questions they write.

Game shows are naturally funny because any time you have people who don't know the answer to something, hilarity usually ensues. But game shows that are designed to create laughter—think *Family Feud, Let's Make a Deal, The Newlywed Game,* and *Are You Smarter Than a 5th Grader?*—are an easy way to double up on the comedy. There's a reason so many stand-up comedians host these types of programs.

Directions Create an equal number of groups of four to five players. Each team will create its own game show, writing questions and answers, and deciding what format the game will take. Generally speaking, game shows can be divided into five categories:

1. dare shows [contestants choose between a question and a dare]
2. fake celebrities provide funny possible answers, and the contestant tries to choose the right one
3. contestants guess the answers to silly questions
4. players try to show how much they know about people with whom they are close [parents, spouse, boss, siblings, etc.]
5. dating games that try to match people

Allow groups twenty minutes to create a show and write ten or more questions. When the time is up, one player from one group will be the host of that group's show, while players from another team will be the contestants. After the game is played, the groups switch roles.

Tips

- Silly questions create more laughter than serious questions.
- Games that involve both questions and physical elements create more opportunities for laughs.

64 It's Not Magic

Props A top hat, a deck of cards, a cardboard box big enough for someone to fit inside, a pitcher, a coin, and any other usual magic props. Other useful things include a variety of stuffed animals, toys, duct tape (duct tape always comes in handy), and random items that players can use to add humor to their tricks.

Magic and comedy have one major similarity—you shouldn't be able to guess what's going to happen before it does. Magic shows are usually funny only when something goes wrong. But what if the tricks themselves were funny instead of mysterious? This game lets players toy with the idea of using magic for laughs.

Directions Create pairs of players and provide each with the list of questions below. Each pair should spend five minutes deciding on the funniest answers and another five minutes to come up with a way to perform one or more of the tricks, with one player serving as the magician and the other playing the magician's assistant.

1. What would be funnier than a rabbit coming out of a hat?
2. Instead of disappearing, someone steps into a box and what happens?
3. It's hard to levitate or float above the ground. What could a bad magician do instead?
4. Everyone's seen the trick in which a magician pretends to pour milk down his pants. What would happen if instead of milk, she poured something else?
5. Someone steps behind a box or a curtain and instead of immediately reappearing in a different outfit, what happens?
6. Sawing people in half has been done. How else could the trick go?

Tips

- A wisecracking magician's assistant is a good way to up the humor ante.
- Funny "magic words" add another element of comedy.

65 A Day in the Life of a Vampire

Props In addition to generic props, a vampire cape and teeth can make this game more "realistic"

Why should vampires have all the fun? Think about it—they're always living in castles, fighting epic battles, and falling in love. But what are their lives like during their off hours? This game allows players to create funny sketches exploring those possibilities.

Directions Create groups of three to four players and give them ten minutes to write a sketch in which a vampire or vampires do normal everyday stuff such as brush their teeth, shop for groceries, do laundry, or meet with junior's principal at school. Each sketch should include a part for every player in the group. When writing time is up, allow the groups ten minutes to rehearse, and then it's fangs on!

Tips

- Including average, nonvampire characters in the scene helps make things funnier.
- Vampires always seem so cool and suave. A bumbling, inarticulate batty creature can get more giggles.

66   Fast and Funny Movies

Props   A prop box; access to the Internet

We all have favorite movies; some of us even regularly quote lines originally spoken by our movie's actors. This game creates fun and laughter by having players act out their favorite movie in five minutes.

Directions   Create groups of three to five players and ask each group to choose a movie they'd like to act out in three minutes. Steer players, especially boys and young men, away from violent flicks. A list of some movies that work well is provided below. If not everyone in each group is entirely familiar with the movie chosen, encourage players to log on to the IMDb website and review the characters and storyline. Wikipedia is also a good place to find summaries of movie stories.

Movies That Work Well in 5 Minutes (for Kids and Grown-Ups)

Black Beauty	How the Grinch Stole Christmas	The Sound of Music
Finding Nemo		Spiderman
Footloose	The Little Mermaid	Willy Wonka
Harry Potter (any & all)	Princess Bride	
	Shrek	

Movies That Work Well in 5 Minutes (Just for Grown-Ups)

Casablanca	Jaws	Star Wars
Gone with the Wind	Raiders of the Lost Ark	Thelma & Louise
It's a Wonderful Life	The Rocky Horror Picture Show	When Harry Met Sally

Give the groups ten minutes to write a three-page script that includes all the members of the group. The script should not be a scene from the movie; it should be the entire movie encapsulated. Allow another ten minutes for players to rehearse their lines, and then it's premiere time.

Tips
- Performing the movie in fast forward ups the comedy potential.
- If the chosen movie does not have enough roles for the entire group, one player can do the background music and another can do sound effects.

Variation   Two groups do the same movie and share a laugh at how each approached things differently.

67 Funny Scary Stories

A group of kids and adults sit around a campfire making S'mores when something rustles the bushes nearby. It sounds big and scary. The kids scream. The grown-ups pretend to be brave, but their eyes are wide, and their hearts pump wildly. Just as one of the adults is about to head toward the bushes with a flashlight and a burning marshmallow.... How does it end? Only the players in this game can tell us.

Directions Form groups of two to three players and ask them to write a typical campfire story that builds tension and suspense and makes everyone think something horrible will happen. Just when the scariest part should come, the players will write a funny ending instead.

Give the groups ten minutes to write their stories and another five minutes to rehearse how they will be told. Then have all the players sit in a circle on the ground and let the stories commence.

Tips

- Sound effects can help build tension.
- Scary stories are always better when told slowly and with deliberation.

68 Video Game Game

Props A prop and costume box; a pair of dice

Video games—some people (mostly male people) love them and some (mostly mothers and teachers) hate them. They've been blamed for everything from obesity to violence. But Video Game Game allows players to write their own nonviolent game in which players from another group have to do the actions instead of sitting on the sofa eating chips and ice cream. What's not to love?

Directions Create two teams of equal numbers and explain to them that the goal of this game is to write a unique, noncombatant video game that the other team will have to act out. As with most video games, the game each team creates should have obstacles, rewards, punishments, magical elements, and most of all, fun written into the script. Each game must include a role for each of the players on the opposite team.

This is a really fun sketch-writing game especially for teens, so allow plenty of time—an hour would not be too much—for the players to work. Encourage teams to first establish the goal of their video game. Is it to get to the stranded platypus first, to eat the most kiwi fruit without dropping any, to escape from work to another planet without anyone noticing, or...? Once the goal is established, it becomes much easier to write the instructions for actions that the players on the other team will have to act out. A sample fill-in-the-blank list of actions may be found below.

Sample Actions for Video Game Game

- A _____ appears, and it _____.
- A _____ touches you from behind, and you _____.
- The _____ beneath you starts to _____.
- The sound of _____ rings out from the _____.
- Two _____ run in front of you and ask for _____.
- When you reach for the _____, _____ happens.
- While walking toward _____, you fall into _____.
- You feel _____, so you go to _____.
- You lose your _____ and have to _____.
- You must jump over _____.
- You round the corner and are faced with _____.

- You smell _____ and suddenly _____.
- You take a bite of _____ and _____.

When time is up, each team chooses a leader who will read the script one action at a time as the other team takes the stage and acts out the game.

Tip Characters should have funny names and odd powers.

Variations

- Instead of being played as written in the script, each "action" may be written on a card and the opposite team rolls a pair of dice to see what next action has to be taken.
- Once the game has been played, players from both teams may be encouraged to add to or change certain elements to make the games funnier the next time around.

Improv Comedy

Improv comedy can be scary because you are working without a net: There is no script and no time to gather ideas about how you might act out a scene. You just jump into things and hope for the best. Of all the comedy styles, it's the closest to bungee jumping.

For these same reasons, improv can be the source of the biggest laughs. I've taught all types of comedy games for more years than I believe is possible and the thigh-slapping-est, bent over at the waist giggling-est, can't catch my breath because I'm snort-laughing-est moments happen more often and more quickly during improv than during any other form of comedy. Perhaps it is because with improv, everyone has to drop the idea of being the best and just settle for being a five-year-old again—no egos, no judgments, no time for the inner critics to criticize every move. It's amazing what happens when we play so freely. It's no coincidence that many of the funniest and most successful comedians and comedy writers have their roots in improv, including Stephen Colbert, Tina Fey, Amy Poehler, Eugene Levy, John Belushi, and Jane Lynch, just to name a few.

The two most important elements of improv comedy are: (1) jump in and do it; don't sit back and wait for a brilliant idea, and (2) always keep in mind the principal of "Yes, and." This means that when another player takes the scene in a certain direction, you go with it, not against it. This is why improv is such a great tool for teaching kids and grown-ups to play well with others—we actually have to pay attention to them and work together to achieve a good (funny) result. What a concept!

If you would like to explore more improv games, I recommend *101 Improv Games for Children and Adults* and *101 More Improv Games for Children and Adults*, both by Bob Bedore, a member of the well-known improv troupe Quick Wits.

A quick note: Some games in this section are marked with the physical contact icon because they require players to be comfortable in close proximity, but all improv games have the potential to end up involving lots of physical contact, depending upon how players act out the scenes.

69 This to That

It's boring to be stuck being yourself all the time. This game allows players to explore the comedic potential of change.

Directions One player at a time will take the stage, ready to play. Encourage the group to call out one thing for the player to be and another for her to change into. To jump-start the game, a list of possibilities appears below. Remind players that this game isn't about being one thing and then the other but, rather, about transitioning from the one to the other. At one point, each player will have characteristics of both the thing she was and the thing she is becoming.

From This...	to That...	From This...	to That...
baby	teenager	parent	child
banana	monkey	poor	rich
bear	lamb	Shakespeare	Shakira
car	carp	sloth	greed
cat	bat	teapot	espresso machine
clown	principal	tiny	huge
egg	chicken	tree	coffee table
happy	paranoid	triangle	circle
light bulb	lightning	wet	dry
man	woman		

Tips

- This game is more fun when played slowly; there is no need to rush the transition.
- The more physical action, the better.
- Choosing a midpoint in the room by which each player will be halfway through her transition can help.

Variations

- Two players may do the same transformation from this to that at the same time.
- Once the transformation has occurred, the players may transform back.

70 Well, That's Unexpected

One of my favorite scenes in *The Princess Bride* is when Wesley and Buttercup have to cross the fire swamp in the middle of the forest. There's something inherently funny about having to deal with someone unexpected along the path, and this game lets players explore different funny options for going around, through, over, and under unusual imaginary objects they encounter.

Directions Have the entire group decide upon something that would be unusual to find in the middle of the sidewalk or road, such as a UFO, a giraffe, a gingerbread house, or a black hole. Invite the players one at a time to cross the room, stumble upon the object, and deal with it. Each player much choose an approach different from those who have gone before.

Tips

- Body language, facial expressions, and words all help convey a funny story while playing this game.
- As long as players are imagining something in their path, there's no reason it has to be found in its usual manner. For example, perhaps a giraffe is balanced on a fence post or driving a car.

Variation Two players work together to deal with the unexpected obstacle.

71 I'm Sorry, But...

When I was fourteen, the movie *Love Story* hit the big screens. Anyone who saw it remembers its most famous quote: "Love means never having to say you're sorry." Of course, that's not really true, and life is filled with times when we must say "I'm sorry." This improv game explores the humor potential in apologies for all sorts of misdeeds.

Directions Form two equal groups of players and have them stand in two single-file lines so that the first player of group #1 faces the first player of group #2. Choose one item from the list of things to apologize for (below) and ask each player to start a sentence that begins with, "I'm sorry that I..." and ends with a funny excuse. For example: "I'm sorry that I ate your food out of the refrigerator, but I fed mine to the hedgehog." Each player takes a turn and then steps to the end of his line until everyone has had a chance to apologize and provide a funny excuse.

Things to Apologize For: I'm Sorry I...

- ate your food out of the refrigerator
- borrowed your shirt
- drove too fast on the freeway
- knocked down your mailbox with my car
- pretended to be a doctor
- read your mail
- redecorated your house while you were out
- refused to go to the dance with you
- rummaged through your medicine chest
- said your cat was fat
- said something mean about you
- set your lawn on fire
- shaved your head while you were sleeping
- stepped on your toe
- stole your idea and said it was mine
- threw snails in your yard
- took $40 out of your wallet
- unfriended you on Facebook

Tip If players listen closely to the apologies that go before their turn to play, they can use the classic comedy technique called "callback," which builds upon previous jokes. For example, if one player apologizes for eating someone's French fries by saying, "My blood sugar was low," and another says, "The voices in my head made me do it," a callback might be, "The voices in my head had low blood sugar."

72 Weird Thing in the Closet

They say we all have skeletons in our closets, but what about the other weird stuff in there hiding behind the shoes and shirts? In this game, a player discovers something unusual behind the closet door and has to decide how to deal with it. The funnier that "something" is, the more fun the game will be.

Directions This is a two-player game: One player will find something funny and odd in the closet, and the other player will be that "something." Before the game begins, someone in the group will whisper to player #2 exactly what he will be (a list of prompts follows). He takes his place and quietly waits for player #1 to open the closet doors.

Weird Thing in the Closet Ideas

Bigfoot	mermaid	sun
bus driver	NFL football player	teapot
Christmas tree	Old West sheriff	tightrope walker
fairy	Pinocchio	unicorn
giant lizard	pirate	waterfall
leprechaun	plumber	World's largest dust
magician	skeleton	bunny

As the scene plays out, the first player tries to figure out what is in the closet and what to do about it. The second player does not speak but can use body language, facial expressions, and grunting or humming to convey what he represents.

Tips

- If the weird thing in the closet is too easy to identify, the game won't be as much fun.

- If the weird thing is an inanimate object, it should have some obvious characteristics for player #2 to act out.

73 Remember When You...

Sometimes I can't remember what I did five minutes ago, so it's not far-fetched to think that someone could convince me I had done something in the past that I had not. In this game, players get to create their own "new memories"—the funnier, the better.

Directions One player takes center stage and someone else from the group shouts out, "Remember when you..." and then fills in the ending. For example, "Remember when you were the first person to walk on the moon?" or "Remember when you ran off and joined the circus?"

The player on stage then creates a monologue with action recollecting this "event" from his past.

Tips

- "Memories" that have strong physical components are the most fun to reenact.
- Total commitment to having done the thing in the past increases the funny potential.

Variation Two players share the memory and share in telling and acting it out for the rest of the group.

74 Odd Patient/ Bad Therapist

A lot of comedy has been mined from pairing two people who are somehow at odds with each other. Who better for these roles than a therapist who is bad at her job and a patient with a weird problem?

Directions One player is assigned a weird patient condition (a list of suggestions follows), while the other plays the role of a therapist who isn't good at her job. Player #2 may choose to be incompetent in any way she likes—she can ignore the patient, spend the whole "session" talking about her own problems, have a second job she does at the same time, etc. The rest of the players watch and laugh until it is their time to take the stage.

Odd Patient Conditions

Patient believes...

aliens are living in his car

birds hate him

cats speak to him

earth is shaped like a triangle

everything in his house is watching him

the ground is boiling hot

Justin Bieber is stalking him

he is a fax machine

he is invisible

he is the reincarnation of Napoleon

he is starting to sprout horns

his boss is a hologram

squirrels are planning to kidnap him

taking a shower will make him melt

tap dancing will solve global warming

Tips

- "Conditions" should be highly exaggerated for the most laughter.
- The problem does not need to be resolved; in fact, it is funnier if the problem is actually worse at the end of the game.

Variation Play this game as a couples' counseling session, with two people with unique problems and one very bad counselor.

75 Hey! Can You Lend Me a Hand?

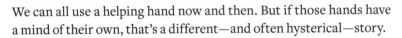

We can all use a helping hand now and then. But if those hands have a mind of their own, that's a different—and often hysterical—story.

Directions This four-player game lets two players play a scene while two other players provide their gestures and other hand and arm movements while standing behind them. The two players who speak tuck their hands in their pockets or behind their backs to avoid using them during the scene.

Once the players and their roles have been determined, give each speaking character a role that requires the use of lots of hand motions and gestures (a list of suggestions follow). Players who are the "helping hands" may either provide hand motions that follow the storyline created by the speaking players or they may create action that requires the speakers to follow along (or both).

Character Ideas for "Hey! Can You Lend Me a Hand?"

acrobat	fortune-teller	skier
ballerina	Indy driver	swimmer
baseball player	jump rope turner	supermodel
Boy Scout/Girl Scout	kite flyer	surgeon
clown	lion tamer	taffy puller
cheerleader	monkey	telephone pole climber
construction worker	pizza maker	

Tips

- Players should be comfortable with each other before playing this game because it requires a lot of physical contact.
- Players of relatively equal height should be paired to make the game easier for everyone.

Variations

- Only one of the speaking players has helping hands.
- The speaking players use one hand and the helpers provide the other.

76 Interview with a Fairy Tale Character

What happens when a television reporter asks Cinderella questions about the fire that broke out at her stepmother's house? Or someone peppers Rumpelstiltskin with questions about some gold missing from a local bank? This game allows players to find out while having lots of laughs along the way.

Directions In this two-player game, one takes on the role of a famous fairy tale character while the other plays a TV news reporter. The pair chooses both the fairy tale character and the news story that is being reported.

Tip The news story doesn't have to be relevant to the fairy tale, but it is often funnier if it is.

Variation The reporter may interview a whole group of characters from one fairy tale to get different takes on the story.

77 Teach a Blank to Blank

This is one of my favorite games. It puts players in an impossible situation, and the laughs just don't stop.

Directions Two players take the stage: One will be the "teacher," and the other will be something or someone who is hard to teach. The rest of the group decides what type of animal or character the student should be and what the teacher must teach her to do—the more outrageous the combination, the better. Here is a list of ideas for both the character and the activity.

"Teach a Blank to Blank" Prompts

alligator to retrieve tennis balls

anteater to dust

basketball player to be a jockey

cat to retrieve slippers

dog to purr

giraffe to do the limbo

kindergartner to roof houses

koala bear to fry an egg

leprechaun to play basketball

octopus to knit

poodle to drive

porcupine to do acupuncture

rhinoceros to dance ballet

snake to do sit-ups

squirrel to mow grass

swordfish to chop vegetables

starfish to surf

Tips

- Although the teaching role doesn't seem as much fun to play, it drives the comedy in this game.
- Players may switch roles after their scene is finished.

78 My Lips Are Sealed

Who hasn't been told not to talk with his mouth full? That may be good rule of etiquette and polite dining behavior, but in this game players chew through some laughs by expressing themselves without opening their mouths.

Directions In this two-player game, one player acts out a scene with another who must pretend her mouth is full and the only way she can communicate is by talking with her lips closed.

The player who speaks clearly acts as if she understands everything. For example, if player #2 mumbles a sentence, player #1 might respond, "But we had Chinese food last night. It's my turn to pick!" as if she heard and understood every word. The speaking player will direct the action because she interprets everything and moves the scene forward.

Tip In this game, tone, facial expression, and body language are really important for the nonspeaking player.

79 Opposites Stuck in an Elevator

This is another fun improv game that creates laughter by mismatching characters. In this case, personalities that are polar opposites find themselves in a situation in which they have to work together to achieve a goal.

Directions Two players are given characters who are the opposite of each other. Some suggested characters are provided in the list below. The players act out the scene as if they are stuck in an elevator together, trying to get out. They can choose whether or not their characters eventually get out.

Opposite Characters

angry person and happy person

neatnik and slob

country folk and city folk

coward and risk taker

extrovert and introvert

fashionista and sloppy dresser

speedy person and slow-poke

goody two-shoes and criminal

hard worker and slacker

loud person and quiet person

macho man and helpless woman

optimist and pessimist

techie and technophobe

vegetarian and carnivore

very old person and very young person

Tip The stronger the differences between the characters, the funnier the game is.

Variation This game may be played with three characters: two with opposite personalities, and one who tries to find a happy middle ground between them.

80 Two Words/Ten Words

Much of the comedy that comes from improv is the result of setting up obstacles for characters and seeing how they deal with them. That's why improv is such great training for life; it helps everyone learn to find solutions and laugh along the way. This game restricts how many words at a time players can use when speaking.

Directions Two players volunteer to act out a scene suggested by the rest of the group. One player is allowed to talk in only two-word sentences; the other must talk in ten-word sentences. The wordier player may use his fingers to keep track of his words.

The goal is to play the game as if these restrictions are completely normal; it's just that one character is reticent and the other is more talkative.

Tips

- When played with groups that include both younger and older players, the younger players should be assigned the shorter sentences so they don't have to try to keep track of their words.

- Players should try to avoid counting syllables, which often happens accidentally.

Variation The game may be played with three and eleven words or four and twelve words. Any more words than these amounts, and it becomes difficult for the player counting to keep track.

81 Movie Character in Another Movie

What if Chewbacca showed up in *Gone with the Wind* or Romeo wound up in *Bridesmaids*? This game uses just such movie character mix-ups to create laughs.

Directions In this three-person game, two of the players take the stage as stars in a movie chosen by the group. The third person comes in after a few lines, as a specific character from another, seemingly incompatible, movie.

The introduction of the out-of-place character changes the first movie. Remind players that they are the characters in the movie and not actors, so they don't ask the odd person out what he is doing there but instead just move forward as if a monkey wrench hasn't just been thrown into the script.

Tips

- The odder the pairing of movie and out-of-place character, the better.
- Players don't have to know the movie scene by scene; the addition of the odd characters tends to change the script quickly anyway.

Musical Comedy

Music and comedy go together like peanut butter and jelly (although you should probably never eat a PB&J sandwich before singing or trying to be funny on stage!). The ability to combine two very entertaining art forms at the same time has launched the careers of many funny people, from Steve Martin to Bette Midler to Garfunkel and Oates. And just think of all the laughs musical comedy movies such as *Hairspray, Little Shop of Horrors, A Funny Thing Happened on the Way to the Forum,* and *The Rocky Horror Picture Show* have created for decades.

The great thing about having fun with musical comedy is that it doesn't require much musical skill. Even people without a treasure trove of singing, dancing, or instrumental talent can boost their funny by incorporating a little song parody, a few notes on a kazoo, or some odd soft-shoe dance across the stage. The games in this section focus on using music for comedy's sake.

82 Too-Fast Sing-Along

Props Printed lyrics from a song or songs with which you don't think your players will be familiar, but that you know well enough to lead. Make sure the song(s) you choose are appropriate to the age of your players.

One of the main reasons so many people enjoy karaoke is that they know they're going to get to watch a lot of people screw up well-known songs. A fun night of karaoke is as much about the laughter as the music. This game ensures musical mishaps of another sort.

Directions Distribute one sheet of lyrics to every three to four players so that they have to work together as a group. Explain that everyone is going to sing the song together, one time at its regular speed and then faster and faster.

Sing the song to the group to familiarize players with it. It doesn't matter that they won't really learn the music right away; that helps boost the funny in the game. Immediately after you finish singing, lead everyone through the song at a normal rate of speed. Give them a few seconds and then have everyone sing the song with you at double speed. Try to speed it up once more. You want to get to the point where it's impossible for anyone, including you, to keep up and get the lyrics right. That's when the laughter really starts.

Tips

- One to two verses of a song are enough for this activity.
- Standing on a chair while serving as choir director helps you keep everyone on pace.

Variation Incorporate a little choreography so that as the song speeds up, the actions also become impossible to follow.

83 Parody, Sweet Parody

Props It might be helpful to have online access to retrieve song lyrics and also be able to utilize an online rhyming dictionary.

Just as with cliché jokes (described in Game #27, That's So Cliché), song parodies derive much of their humor from the fact that the audience is familiar with the song and expects specific lyrics to be sung. Different and funny lyrics—such as when Michael Jackson's "Beat It" became Weird Al's "Eat It"—create incongruity and laughter.

Directions Create groups of three to four players and give them fifteen minutes to take a song they all know and write new lyrics to it. Encourage the players to write down the original lyrics first, so they can play around with changing them. Each team works on a different song.

After the songwriting time is up, allow another five minutes for the groups to rehearse the tune. Then invite all the members of each team to sing their creation together in front of the rest of the players.

Tips

- Songs that tell a story are easier to parody.
- The rhyming word list from Game #30, I Am Spam; Spam I Am, can be useful in this game as well.

Variations

- Have all teams write new lyrics to the same original song.
- If someone in the group plays an instrument, encourage her to play along as her team performs.

84 Singin' in the Blank

Even people too young to know who Gene Kelly was have probably seen the iconic song and dance number, "Singin' in the Rain" from the movie of the same name. Kelly was an amazing dancer, and the song has a delightful concept, both of which have helped this number remain popular for more than sixty years. This game puts a spin on the idea but uses odd songs and poor dance moves to focus on the comedy.

Directions Create groups of three to four players, each of which will write a silly song with a title that begins with "Singin' in the..." and ends with a place or situation from the list that follows. Before the groups begin writing their song lyrics (which may use existing music or be completely original), let the players know that they will also be choreographing a bad dance number for the song in which all players in their group will participate.

Places/Circumstances in Which to Sing

box	school
bridge	shopping cart
cave	snow
elevator	Spain
hailstorm	submarine
locker	tree
Mars	tub
moon	wind
plane	yard
pool	zoo
restaurant	

Tips

- Song lyrics that convey motion and action make choreographing dance moves easier.

- Jotting down a list of things associated with the location of the song can help players come up with more ideas. For example, for a song called, "Singin' in the Cave," the list might include: dark, cold, bats, stalactites, stalagmites, bears, gold, water, etc.

85   Rap the Menu

Props Take-out menus from a variety of different types of restaurants

Take some words that rhyme and a recurring beat pattern (often provided by a human "beat boxer,") and you have the basics of rap music. Add in a funny concept for a rap song, and you have the basics of hilarity.

Directions Create groups of four to five players and give each group a take-out menu. Give the groups five minutes to determine who will be the rapper, who will do the beat box, and who will dance hip-hop in the background. The rapper will be responsible for making up lyrics on the spot, using the menu as a jumping off point.

When prep time is up, invite groups to take the stage and rap their menu.

Tips

- This game may be easier for kids and teens than for adults, but there's almost nothing funnier than watching middle-aged folks trying to rap.

- Rap songs that integrate the dialect that reflects the nationality of the restaurant can create extra fun.

Variation Rather than rapping, players may write a song in a genre that is incongruous with their menu. Consider using a polka song about Japanese food or a country song about Italian dishes, for example.

86 The "I Love You" Song

Paul McCartney once crooned, "Some people want to fill the world with silly love songs." So why not add a few more that are truly silly and outrageous to the mix?

Directions Invite one player at a time to take center stage with the instructions that the rest of the group will toss out something to which he must pledge his undying love in a song. Suggest to the group that they choose everyday things that are easy to rhyme with (a list of possible topics follows).

I Love...

air	cheese	feet	sleep
my bed	clothes	fire	socks
blues	dance	myself	spring
cats	dogs	rain	Twitter

Once player #1 has finished crooning, the rest of the players take a turn one at a time, singing their love for something different each time.

Tips

- The more in the moment and unplanned a player is, the better for this game.
- What's a song without a little choreography?

Variation Two players sing the song as a duet.

87 Whose National Anthem Is That?

Who among us, including many celebrities, hasn't struggled to hit the correct notes and remember the proper lyrics to "The Star-Spangled Banner"? Let's face it: it's not the easiest song to pull off, especially for those of us who are partly tone deaf or can't hit that high note unless someone is goosing us from behind. So why not write a new anthem and sing it loud and proud?

Directions Form groups of three to four players and give them fifteen minutes to write a new national anthem that highlights some of the funnier things about the United States. When they've finished writing, invite each group to take center stage and perform their song together, along with any choreography they feel is appropriate.

Tip Making a list of funny things about America can make the songwriting easier.

Variations

- Each group writes for a different country.
- Each group writes for a different state.

Prop Comedy

Most people don't put comics such as Carrot Top or Gallagher on their list of favorite comedians, but if you ask me, prop comics get a bad rap. I can say from experience that a room full of people will laugh long and loud at a funny hat or an ostrich puppet or a watermelon being smashed to smithereens or anything else they didn't expect to show up on stage at that given moment.

It makes sense that we laugh at prop comedy. As young kids, we love playing make believe with toys, costumes, and everyday items from around the house. And although as we get older, we don't often dress up or play, the joy of using our imaginations to make up stories that involve "toys" (which is really what props are when used for fun) never really fades.

The games in this section are all improvisational, so they take less time than the games in the "Comedy Writing" and "Sketch Comedy" sections of this book. They rely on a well-stocked prop and costume box (some of them requiring specific items), but it is easy to put one together by collecting items from around the house, at garage sales and second-hand stores, and even asking players to bring their own props in for specific games.

88 In My Country, This Is...

Props Everyday item or items from around the house

If you live in a country where people have never seen a spatula or a shower curtain ring, their idea of how these things will be used may be quite different from ours. And whenever things are unexpected, laughter isn't far behind.

Directions Seat players in a semicircle and hand one everyday item to the first player to volunteer. He will take the item to center stage and begin a monologue with "In my country, this is..." and fill in the blank with a funny use for the prop. Each player in turn will take the same item and create a new use for it in her country. Because each player is from another real or imaginary country, encourage everyone to use an accent for that country.

When everyone has had a turn with the first prop, bring in one or two more, with each player continuing to pretend to be from the same country that they imagined in the first round.

Tips

- Items should be big enough for everyone in the audience to see easily.
- If bringing things from home, avoid breakables.

Variation This can be played with two players who talk about the use of the item together, perhaps agreeing upon its use... or not.

89 Dress Me!

Props Unusual hats; costumes; and accessories (think big, bold, bright, and quirky)

Ask any parent of a child from three to eight years old what his favorite game is and chances are that "dress up" is near the top of the list. Kids love putting on costumes and then creating mini-plays based upon their outfits. The growing popularity of Halloween proves that adults like dressing up almost as much. This game gives everyone an excuse to dress up and pretend.

Directions Have two players at a time take the stage. Hand the players two different costume pieces each. Once they've gotten dressed, ask them to become a character suggested by each of their outfits. Let the rest of the players suggest a scene that works for those characters.

Rinse, lather, repeat...oh, wait...just repeat until everyone has had a turn.

Tip Costumes that don't seem to fit together (i.e., cowboy boots and an astronaut helmet) make for the funniest scenes.

Variations

- Ask the players who aren't in the game to give the players a scene in which their characters seem most out of place.
- Play the game with three players at a time.

90 Model/Photographer

It may not be intended to be comedic, but I've gotten many a laugh while watching *America's Next Top Model*—primarily because the photographers and directors give the models such odd assignments: Pose with an octopus in your hair, hold this owl, let us spray paint you and pretend you are a statue.... So thanks, Tyra Banks, for the idea for this game.

Props Lots of clothing and accessories; a digital camera or cell phone with a camera

Directions Choose half the players to be the models and ask another one to be a photographer. Each model will put together an unusual outfit of his or her choosing, and the photographer will direct a shoot, using one, some, or all of the models at any time. She will ask the models to do unusual poses or walk down an imaginary runway in a quirky way. The goal is for models and photographer to get the funniest shots possible.

After about five minutes, let the other half of the players play the game. When they've all finished, show the photos on the camera or cell phone and let each group choose the ones they think are funniest.

Tips

- Girls generally enjoy this game more than boys; that goes for women and men as well. But having male models makes for a really fun game.
- Both facial expressions and body movement are really important for creating comedy.

Variation Model and photographer are given a "campaign"—such as toothpaste, shampoo, or lawnmowers—to work on.

91 Can I Get a Patent?

Props Any odd items that can be repurposed; the sky (and your pocketbook) is the limit. Examples: cardboard tubes, wire hangers, pieces of scrap metal or plastic, parts of an old radio, zippers, basketballs that don't hold air anymore, broken Frisbees, plastic food containers, springs, rubber bands, paper clips, etc. You need enough stuff for each group of players to have five to seven things for their "invention."

What's the difference between an inventive genius and a comedy genius? That's a hard question to answer because Einstein and Mel Brooks probably have a lot more in common than most people think! This game explores the comedic side of invention and although nothing may end up getting patented, the laughs will be priceless.

Directions Dump your box of assorted odd items on a table and spread them out. Let the players know that this game requires them to put on their best inventor caps to create a unique and funny product that will bring more laughter to the world.

Create teams of three to five players and give them each ten minutes to come up with an idea for their product and what it does. When the time is up, invite each team to work together as a group to try to sell their new invention to the rest of the players.

Tip A funny product name and slogan are bonuses.

Variations

- Players in the audience may be encouraged to ask questions.
- After each team has presented a product, another team may take the same product and sell it as something else.

92 Wiggin' Out

Props A variety of odd wigs

Maybe it's not the clothes but, rather, the hair that makes man and woman. Think of all the famous funny people who are known for their interesting "do's" or their odd wigs: Steven Wright, Emo Phillips, Phyllis Diller, Madeline Kahn in *Young Frankenstein*, etc. This game not only relies on funny wigs, but it also sets out to prove that if you're going to flip your wig, you might as well have a good laugh doing it.

Directions Two players put on wigs and are given a scene to improvise as a character they think suits their new "do." Once they've played the scene through to the end, they switch wigs and do the scene again, repeating everything as close to the first time as possible but playing each other's parts.

Tip Characters with distinct personalities (e.g., old and young, male and female, smart and dumb) make this game more fun when the big switch happens.

Variations

- The players switch wigs and roles halfway through the scene, and instead of recreating the scene, they just move it forward.
- Three players play, doing the scene three times, once as each character.

93 Moustaches and Tiaras

Props Press-on moustaches; a few inexpensive tiaras; a mirror

Put on a moustache, and you feel manly. Put on a tiara, and the opposite happens. The $64,000 question is: What happens when players do both at the same time?

Directions Invite a player to put on a moustache (a fresh press-on moustache for each player is the most hygienic approach) and a tiara. Have the members of the group suggest something that the player is thinking about doing, such as getting married or running a marathon. The player will take the stage and create a monologue on that topic.

Encourage the player in the moustache and tiara to take a good look at herself in the mirror and come up with a character that would look like she does (a woman under a witch's spell that makes her grow facial hair, for example) before playing out the scene.

Tips

- Pairing a crazy voice with the character will make the scene funnier.
- The monologue can be done as a phone conversation, into a mirror, or as something yelled at someone else through an imaginary door.

Variation The player may play two different characters, one represented by the moustache and the other by the tiara, having a conversation with each other.

94 Now What?

Prop A prop box

We all know the old saying, "When life hands you lemons, make lemonade." Or as I always say, "When life hands you lemons, make lemon meringue pie, hit yourself in the face with it, and then laugh along with everyone else." But what do you do if life hands you an alarm clock, a scented candle, and a dog whistle? This game explores the endless funny possibilities.

Directions Two players are given a scene that is suggested by the rest of the group. As they play out the scene, the players in the audience toss props toward them, each of which must then be integrated into the scene. Either one or both players can use each prop.

Scenes should last no more than three minutes because any longer and the play space will be littered with props.

Tips

- Nonplayers should toss props at players' feet, not their heads.
- Add no more than one prop every thirty seconds.

Variations

- Three players can play this game.
- Those audience members tossing the props may call out in what manner they should be used. For example, when tossing a towel, someone may say, "To wipe the sweat off your brow."

95 Human Props

Maybe you've worn a lampshade on your head at a party or had someone mistake you for a coat rack. If so, you've been a human prop. But a human can make himself useful in so many more ways, as this game proves.

Directions This game requires four players: Two of them act out a scene suggested by the audience, and two of them stand by waiting to be used as props. Assign one human prop to each player. Remind the "props" that they cannot move on their own; they must wait to be moved into positions by the talking players.

Tips

- Players should be comfortable touching each other before attempting this game.
- Smaller players make really good props because they are easier to move.
- Scenes that require a variety of "tools" work best (e.g., baking, working on a ranch, building robots).

Variation When the scene has been completed, the human props switch roles with the talking players and play the scene again in their own way, using their own human props.

96 See the Prop; Be the Prop

Prop A prop box

It's one thing to play with toys, but it takes another level of imagination to become them.

Directions Two players act out a scene chosen by the rest of the group. After the scene has started, each player is given a prop that he must now turn, or morph, into, all the while continuing the scene.

For example, let's say the scene involves one character giving another a parking ticket. The players act it out for a minute or so, and then one is given a top hat and the other a yoyo. The top hat attempts to write the ticket out but has no hands with which to do so. He may also take on an English accent or start to dance around. The yo-yo bounces up and down, trying to confuse the top hat and make him forget that he was writing a ticket.

Tip The players continue to talk, despite having become inanimate objects.

97 Head Puppet Theater

Props Two plain black stocking caps; several sets of large peel-and-stick googly eyes; a stage or platform at least six-inches high

Talk about a game that turns things around! By getting a view of the world from the perspective of an upside down cake, players and the audience will be head over heels with laughter.

Directions Two players attach two googly eyes to their chins and place stocking caps on their heads, pulling them down far enough to cover their eyes and nose. The rest of the group comes up with a topic for them to talk about with each other about.

Once the topic has been suggested, the players lie on the stage with their heads over the edge so that their googly eyes are now where their eyes would normally be, their mouths appear upside down, and the top of their heads appear to be black beards. They discuss their topic in this position, using no gestures or body movements.

Tip Choose the scene before the players lie down and make sure it is short so that players don't get neck strain.

Variation Players may also use their arms and hands.

98 How Did This Get Here?

Props Props specific to genres, such as Western, sci-fi, historical, musical, etc.

This game uses the same concept as Game #81, Movie Character in Another Movie, only instead of an out-of-place character, it is an incongruous prop that creates the amusing mix-up.

Directions Two players are given a genre-specific scene, such as "two pioneers crossing the country with Lewis and Clark." The rest of the group chooses one prop that would be unlikely in that scene for each player. For example, in the above scene, a magic wand and a ukulele would be good choices. The players must play the scene using the out-of-place props.

Tip Discourage boys from making every scene a shoot-out by not including weapons in the prop box.

Variations

- Also include costumes from incongruous genres.
- Three players may play the game, using three props.

99 Prop Story

Prop A prop box

It's hard enough to carry out a funny monologue, but having your train of thought interrupted by other people showing up with unusual props is rife with comedy potential.

Directions This game is similar to Game #94, Now What?, except that instead of a multiplayer scene, it is performed as a monologue with assistants.

Ask for both a volunteer and some suggestions for a topic she will discuss with the audience. Once the topic is chosen, choose three other players who will arrive separately during the monologue, holding or wearing a prop. The player must include the prop in the next sentence of the monologue, and the player who arrived with the prop must act out that sentence.

Here is an example:

> *I love spaghetti. It's fun to eat and so messy.* [Enter player carrying suitcase.] *In fact, sometimes I carry a suitcase filled with spaghetti everywhere I go just so I can make sure I can have it when I get hungry.* [Exit first player. Enter second player carrying a stethoscope.] *The best way to tell if spaghetti is done is to listen to it with a stethoscope.* [Exit second player. Enter third player carrying a picture frame.] *I love spaghetti so much I have a picture of it in a frame on my desk. I may just marry spaghetti.*

Tip Props that don't fit the scene well create the most laughter.

Variation Players entering the scene with props may add lines that help drive the monologue in a different direction.

100 Clowning Around

Props Clown costumes, big shoes, wigs, hats, and other accessories enough for a few players to use at the same time. It's easy to pick up really bright stuff that works well for this game at garage sales. I've found overly large shoes at secondhand stores for very little money. In order to have the most fun, it would also pay to have long balloons, a dishwasher-sized cardboard box, and a tricycle on hand.

Clowns are the chopped liver of comedy—many in the comedy field don't find them funny at all, but the act of clowning involves many of the best comedic skills, from funny facial expressions, to physical comedy, to using props. Perhaps it's the make-up that scares people off. So, skip the face paint and send in the clowns anyway.

Directions Before inviting volunteers to play, discuss some of the comedy techniques of clowning: bad juggling; making balloon objects (they don't have to be good to be funny); squeezing into too-small spaces; riding tricycles; the two-clown act in which they alternately try to doff their hats and shake each other's hands; fake slaps and falls; and one part of the body seeming to control another (for example if one clown shakes another's hand, the second clown's opposite leg kicks up). You can find videos of clowning tricks on YouTube.

Divide players into pairs and allow them to practice one or more of the tricks. When everyone is prepared, let players choose costumes and take the stage in pairs to show off their funny clown tricks.

Tips

- Bumbling clowns are funnier than those who seem good at their jobs.
- Facial expressions are very important; without make-up, players have to work even harder to make clown faces.

101 Tribute to Jonathan Winters

Prop A stick about ½ inch in diameter and 18 to 24 inches long

One of the best improv and prop comics was the inimitable Jonathan Winters, who passed away in 2013. To honor him, this game recreates one of his most well-loved bits from *The Jack Paar Show*. Watch the bit on YouTube but don't show it to players because you want them to approach it with their own creativity.

Directions Invite players one at a time to grab the stick and create five short scenes using it. Encourage them to become different characters, perhaps with dialects or specific quirks in each miniscene. Each player should move from one short scene to the next without stopping or thinking.

When player #1 is finished, the next player takes the stick and creates five different scenes and characters.

Tip Players at the beginning have an easier time because someone else won't have already taken their ideas.

Variations

- Two players alternate their miniscenes with the stick.
- Play the same game with another very simple object such as a box or a rope.

Tech Comedy
(Bonus Games)

Well, we've reached 101 comedy games, but I didn't want to leave out a few fun games that can be played using cell phones, tablets, cameras, and other high-tech devices. As technology continues to develop, so do the creative imaginations of people who just want to make the world laugh.

In addition to some of the game ideas provided in this section, you can choose some of your favorite games from the rest of this book and add the extra funny element of technology to them.

102 Sound Effects Machine

Prop A sound effects app on a cell phone or handheld machine (my favorite is a palm-sized machine manufactured by Worldwide Co. that is available online)

There is a classic improv game called "Sound Effects" that relies on having players who are talented at making lots of different kinds of noises with their mouths. Fortunately for those of us who aren't talented at making many different noises, now there are devices that can replicate almost any sound effect so that anyone can play.

Directions Two players are given an improv scene by the rest of the group. As they play the scene, a third player uses a phone sound effects app or a handheld sound effects machine to add sounds to which the players must adapt their scene.

Tips

- Make sure the players are close enough to the sound effects maker to hear the noises as they are made.
- Sound effects shouldn't be interjected more than every 30 seconds or so to allow players to alter the scene in the funniest way possible.

Variations

- Each time a sound effect is played, a new player enters the scene and one of the original players steps out. The scene continues.
- Instead of the sound effects player setting the course of the scene, she must follow the players and create the sound effects they need.

103 Photo Bombing

Prop A camera or camera phone

Although the term "photo bombing" is relatively new, the idea of appearing unexpectedly in a photo, unbeknownst to others, has been around as long as people have been taking pictures. In this game, the fun happens not only when looking at the end result but also in accomplishing it in the first place.

Directions Three players are given an event for which they will be photographed. A fourth is assigned to photo bomb them. The photographer (either you or another player) catches all of this on camera. The goal is to get a photo that is truly funny.

Tip The photographer has to be quick to catch the photo bombing as it happens.

104 Talking Tom Cat App

Props One or more cell phones with the Talking Tom Cat app (free)

What could be funnier than a cat that repeats everything you say?

Directions One player volunteers to perform a monologue with an accent or unique speech style using the Talking Tom Cat app. The cat repeats everything he says.

Tip Short sentences are best so that the player and the cat aren't talking at the same time.

Variations

- A player talks about things as if she is a cat.
- Two players with the same app play a scene.

105 MouthOff App

Props Cell phones with the MouthOff app ($1)

The Eyes Have It (Game #17) and My Lips Are Sealed (Game #78) require players to keep their mouths closed as they play out a scene. MouthOff goes in the other direction, doubling the fun by letting players choose a new mouths and lips to use.

Directions Two players can play any scene from the improv comedy section of this book while holding their cell phone–animated lips in front of their own mouths.

Tip Slow speech, with highly articulated words, makes this game even funnier.

Variation This can be played as a monologue, with the group giving one player a topic to discuss.

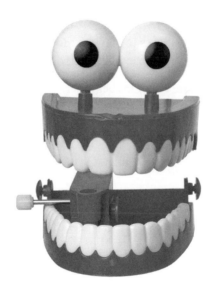

106 Cartoon It!

Props Computers or tablets for each player (have them bring their own from home)

Not everyone can draw well, but anyone can cartoon, especially with all the fun cartooning sites available for free on the Internet. This game allows players to try their hand at turning funny thoughts into funny drawings.

Directions Let players know about free websites that allow them to drop characters, costumes, backgrounds, and thought bubbles into cartoon strips. Some sites to try include:

- Funny Times Cartoon Playground (http://www.funnytimes.com/play ground/#.Uakc5Nhz5hc)
- ToonDoo (http://www.toondoo.com)
- Bitstrips (http://www.bitstrips.com/pageone)
- MakeBeliefsComix (http://www.makebeliefscomix.com/Comix)

Give players 20 to 30 minutes to play around with creating their funniest comic strip and then have them share with the rest of the group.

Tip Three-panel strips are easier for beginners than are one-panel strips.

107 Lights, Camera, Action

Props Video camera; tripod

You've had a ton of fun trying the games in this book; the only problem is you can't share it with the friends and family of your players. Well, with easy access to video cameras and video camera functions on cell phones, there's no reason not to record the laugh-inducing games. Who knows? Maybe yours will be the next viral video.

Directions Have players perform any of the stand-up, sketch, improv, musical, or prop comedy games in this book while the camera records their work.

Tips

- Players need to be aware of and to play to the camera instead of each other.
- In any scene in which part of players' faces are covered, encourage enunciation.

Alphabetical
List of Games

List of Games Arranged by Specific Categories

Games Requiring a Large Space

1. What's Funny About Me
4. Faking It
6. Silly Nonhandshakes
8. Follow the Body Part
13. Duck, Duck, Moose
14. Silly Shambles
21. Bad Exercise Instructor
22. Hop to It
24. So You Think You Can't Dance
67. Funny Scary Stories

Games in Which Physical Contact Might Be Involved

6. Silly Nonhandshakes
12. Stuck on You
13. Duck, Duck, Moose
16. Mirroring
20. Machine
23. Stuck In...
24. So You Think You Can't Dance
64. It's Not Magic
68. Video Game Game
75. Hey! Can You Lend Me a Hand?
90. Model/Photographer
95. Human Props
100. Clowning Around

Games Requiring Props

4. Faking It
5. Funny Audition
7. Voice-Overs
9. Fractured Clichés
10. Words Are Funny
25. Who's That Knocking?
26. Riddle Me This
27. That's So Cliché
28. Read My Bumper
29. The Stories My Bumper Can Tell
30. I Am Spam; Spam I Am
31. The Group Poetry Society
32. Weird Holidays, Weird Cards
33. Then This Happened...
35. Funny Fortune Cookies
36. It Was So Funny.... How Funny Was It?
37. Word Up
38. Why Ask "Why"?
39. What Does Webster Know?
40. You Ought to Have a Motto
41. Insert Caption Here
43. Top Ten Reasons to Do a Top-Ten List
45. First Line/Last Line
47. Half the Script

Photo Copyrights